C0-CEG-663

100 answers to 100 questions

about God's promises for You

100 answers to 100 questions

ask · discover · live smart

about God's promises for You

Christian
LIFE
A STRANG COMPANY

Most CHRISTIAN LIFE products are available at special quantity discounts for bulk purchase for sales promotions, premiums, fund-raising, and educational needs. For details, write Christian Life, 600 Rinehart Road, Lake Mary, Florida 32746, or telephone (407) 333-0600.

100 Answers to 100 Questions About God's Promises for You

Published by Christian Life
A Strang Company
600 Rinehart Road
Lake Mary, Florida 32746

www.strang.com

Scripture quotations marked CEV are from the Contemporary English Version, copyright © 1995 by the American Bible Society. Used by permission.

Scripture quotations marked GNT are from the Good News Translation, Second Edition. Copyright © 1992 by the American Bible Society. Used by permission.

Scripture quotations marked THE MESSAGE are from The Message: *The Bible in Contemporary English*, copyright © 1993, 1994, 1995, 1996, 2000, 2001, 2002. Used by permission of NavPress Publishing Group.

Scripture quotations marked NIV are from the Holy Bible, New International Version. Copyright © 1973, 1978, 1984, International Bible Society. Used by permission.

Scripture quotations marked NLT are from the Holy Bible, New Living Translation, copyright © 1996, 2004. Used by permission of Tyndale House Publishers, Inc., Wheaton, IL 60189. All rights reserved.

Scripture quotations marked NRSV are from the New Revised Standard Version of the Bible. Copyright © 1989 by the Division of Christian Education of the National Council of the Churches of Christ in the USA. Used by permission.

Cover design by Whisner Design Group, Tulsa, Oklahoma

Copyright © 2008 by GRQ, Inc.
All rights reserved

ISBN 10:   1-59979-273-7
ISBN 13:   978-1-59979-273-6

BISAC Category: Religion/Christian Life/General

First Edition

08 09 10 11 12—9 8 7 6 5 4 3 2 1

Printed in the United States of America

I am GOD. . . . I'll stick with you
until I've done everything
I promised you.

Genesis 28:13, 15, THE MESSAGE

Contents

What Are God's Promises for Troubled Times?

What Are God's Promises for Guidance?

What Are God's Promises for the Family?

What Are God's Promises Regarding Prayer?

What Are God's Promises for Peace?

What Are God's Promises for Living the Christian Life?

What Are God's Promises for Shaping Your Character?

Introduction

God has given you the Bible, which is filled with the solutions for every situation in your life. Perhaps you've frantically searched for just the right verse, seeking His promise for a particular circumstance. That is where Bible promise books can be a wonderful help. They list verses that contain God's promises by topic, and they provide a convenient resource for finding verses quickly. But wouldn't it be great if they added some insight on the meaning of the Scriptures and how they apply to your life?

100 Answers to 100 Questions About God's Promises for You will do just that. It is written in an easy-to-understand format that explains the question, clarifies God's promise, and points out how to apply it to your life. You will learn *why* God gave the promise. This unique promise book will give you new understanding as you seek His answers.

God's many promises are thrilling reminders and assurances for you. You have God's personal pledges, and you can rely on them. He has your best interests in mind, whether you are concerned about love, forgiveness, safety, anxiety, finances, right decisions, or turmoil at work. God has a promise that you can lay claim to for every aspect of your life.

100 Answers to 100 Questions About God's Promises for You will fortify your faith and undergird your life with confidence. Read it, take heart, and thank God.

> *In his love he clothes us, enfolds and embraces us; that tender love completely surrounds us, never to leave us.*
> Lady Julian of Norwich
>
> *Abraham never wavered in believing God's promise. In fact, his faith grew stronger, and in this he brought glory to God. He was fully convinced that God is able to do whatever he promises. And because of Abraham's faith, God counted him as righteous. And when God counted him as righteous, it wasn't just for Abraham's benefit. It was recorded for our benefit, too, assuring us that God will also count us as righteous if we believe in him.*
> Romans 4:20–24, NLT

question

What is a covenant promise?

The word *covenant* sounds like a strange, outdated word. This word is used often in the Old Testament section of the Bible. But you're never quite sure what people mean when they talk about God's making a covenant. Perhaps it was something like a verbal contract. Yet when you've heard people talk about certain biblical covenants, they seemed rather one-sided. God seemed to set the rules. Exactly what does God mean by "covenant"?

answer

Sometimes parents have to lay down the law to their children for their own protection or to teach responsibility. A parent might have to tell their school-age child, "If you do your chores throughout the week, then you can have free time on Saturday. If you do not, then you will spend Saturday catching up on your assigned tasks." In essence, the parent is making an agreement with the child to choose to receive either positive or negative consequences. The choice is the child's, and the purpose of that choice is to teach that obedience brings pleasure. The parent has set the terms of the agreement, but the results are based on the child's response.

God's covenants with the Israelites worked in a similar manner and were contingent on certain conditions being met. God desired the best for His people and laid the ground rules for what they needed to do, but the results depended on how the people chose to respond. God stated both the positive consequences of obedience and the negative consequences of disobedience.

God also made unconditional covenants where He promised that something would come to be, and only He had the power to bring it about. In this type of covenant, God made a definite decision and would follow through with His pronouncement. These solemn agreements, the *conditional* and the *unconditional*, were the two types of covenants God made with His chosen people.

worth thinking about

▶ **God is fair** in that He does not leave you blindsided. He states both the positive and the negative consequences of your choices, and then gives you free will to decide how you will live.

▶ **God is like** a loving parent. All of His principles and rules of conduct are to bring good into the lives of His people.

▶ **God is all-powerful** and all-wise. Biblical history has shown God's ability to fulfill His promises. He can be trusted to do what He says He will do.

> I am setting before you today a blessing and a curse—the blessing if you obey the commands of the LORD your God that I am giving you today; the curse if you disobey the commands of the LORD your God.
> Deuteronomy 11:26–28, NIV

question

What covenant promise did God make with Adam?

The creation story of Adam and Eve in the Garden of Eden is a familiar one. God told them not to eat the fruit from a certain tree. If they did, they would die. Satan, in the form of a serpent, tempted Eve to taste the forbidden fruit. She surrendered and enticed Adam to do likewise. Did God make a promise to Adam and Eve after their disobedience? If so, what were the conditions?

answer

Genesis, the first book in the Bible, reveals that God created everything, including man and woman. He placed them in the beautiful Garden of Eden and made a conditional covenant with them regarding this paradise: "You may freely eat the fruit of every tree in the garden— except the tree of the knowledge of good and evil. If you eat its fruit, you are sure to die" (Genesis 2:16–17, NLT).

God had made it clear what would happen if they broke His conditional covenant: death would enter the world. Adam and Eve learned that God always does what He says and means what He says. They broke the covenant, and death entered the world.

God made a second covenant promise with Adam, a promise that was unconditional: The serpent was cursed to crawl on his belly, while weeds and thorns would curse the ground. Adam would struggle to make a living from the soil until his death. Eve would desire her husband, who would be her master. She would bear his children in suffering. The children of the woman and the children of the devil—those who choose evil—would always be enemies. But a future promise of hope was given: good would triumph over evil.

Evil had entered the world, and the consequences have been evident in nature as well as in the lives of men and women. This unconditional covenant is the promise God made with Adam.

worth thinking about

▶ **Temptation is like** a blindfold to the future. It only lets you see the pleasure of the moment.

▶ **Choices, both good** and bad, affect other people. Adam and Eve's decision to eat the forbidden fruit caused death to enter the human race. If they had chosen obedience, the outcome would have been positive.

▶ **God can bring** good out of wrong choices. Even in declaring the consequences of disobedience, He gives hope for the future by declaring that the woman's seed (Jesus) would triumph over Satan.

> *Christ has been raised to life! And he makes us certain that others will also be raised to life. Just as we will die because of Adam, we will be raised to life because of Christ.*
>
> 1 Corinthians 15:20–21, CEV

question

What covenant promise did God make with Noah?

The biblical story of Noah's ark has long been a favorite with many people. Numerous versions have been published in children's storybooks, songs, and movies. Scientists have discovered evidence that a worldwide flood really did occur. Almost every Christian and non-Christian culture has a story about a great flood in its history. The story of the Flood is no doubt true, but you do have questions. Why wasn't Noah afraid it would happen again? Did God make him a promise that it wouldn't?

answer

The world in Noah's day was corrupt. God was filled with disgust over mankind's wickedness, and He decided to destroy the earth and everything and everyone in it with a flood, all accept Noah. God saved Noah because "Noah was a good man, a man of integrity in his community" (Genesis 6:9, THE MESSAGE).

God gave specific directions for building the ark. Obedient Noah must have endured much ridicule because up until the time of the Flood it hadn't rained. Noah's family safely entered the ark and remained there until the floodwaters receded.

After the Flood, God blessed Noah and his sons and gave them instructions for living. They were to have many children and care for the animals. God also demanded capital punishment for a person or animal that killed someone. He instructed them that they could eat the meat of animals, but never to eat the blood. Then God told Noah and his sons, "I establish my covenant with you: Never again will all life be cut off by the waters of a flood; never again will there be a flood to destroy the earth" (Genesis 9:11, NIV).

worth thinking about

▶ **The covenant** took care of any concerns that Noah might have had about God sending another flood. God keeps His promises. God's covenant with Noah and his descendants remains intact today. It is for everyone.

▶ **Life is considered** sacred because God created people in His image. God didn't want the corruption to return; thus, in the covenant with Noah and his descendants, He forbade murder and commanded capital punishment.

▶ **God would rather** bless than destroy. The conditions set forth in the covenant promise with Noah and future generations are for the good of mankind.

> *I will never again curse the ground because of the human race, even though everything they think or imagine is bent toward evil from childhood. I will never again destroy all living things. As long as the earth remains, there will be planting and harvest, cold and heat, summer and winter, day and night.*
>
> Genesis 8:21–22, NLT

question

What is the covenant promise of the rainbow?

The beauty of a rainbow after a storm is breathtaking. Even the story of Noah's ark has the rainbow appearing after the Flood. People have always had a fascination with the rainbow, and countless myths and stories have centered on it. When you were a kid, you and your friends tried to run toward the rainbow's end in hopes of finding a treasure. Now you realize that the treasure was found only in fairy tales. But is there a promise connected to the rainbow?

answer

The real truth regarding the rainbow is found in Genesis, chapter 9. All other stories of the rainbow or its treasure are just that—stories. God placed the rainbow in the clouds after the Flood. The rainbow is a sign of the eternal covenant, a promise that God made with Noah and his descendants, and it still is applicable to your life today. God will never completely destroy the earth or its inhabitants by sending another flood as He did in Noah's day.

Because life is a constant mix of sunshine and rain and of good and evil, the appearance of the rainbow is a covenant reminder. God said that when the rainbow appears in the clouds, He will remember His promise. But the rainbow serves as a reminder and a comfort for you, too. You are reminded of God's promised blessings to Noah and his descendants, including you.

God's covenant promise never to destroy you can be applied to your personal life. He will not let your storms of trials destroy you. You can trust that He will bring you through your storm and pour out His blessings upon you. God's goal has always been to save mankind, and the rainbow is His sign that He will keep His promise.

worth thinking about

▶ **Handwriting is unique** to each person, and the rainbow is God's unique handwriting. It is His signature. He used the flourish of the science He created to seal His promise to mankind.

▶ **The rainbow** is like a compass pointing to the reason why Jesus would come to earth. God desires to save you.

▶ **The rainbow is** a constant assurance that God will keep His covenant promise. If you grow fearful in any kind of storm—physical, emotional, or spiritual—remember that God will not fail you. He placed His sign high up in the clouds so that you would not forget how much He loves you.

> *The rainbow that I have put in the sky will be my sign to you and to every living creature on earth. It will remind you that I will keep this promise forever.*
> Genesis 9:12–13, CEV

question

What covenant promise did God make with Abraham?

History teaches that Abraham was one of the patriarchs of biblical times. He was also an important man to God. His wife's name was Sarah, and they had a son in their old age. But how did Abraham please God? Why is his name mentioned so frequently in talking about faith? What major role did he play in biblical history? Did God make a covenant promise with Abraham? If so, what was it, and does it have any meaning for your life?

answer

God made a covenant with Abraham: "Leave your country, your people and your father's household and go to the land I will show you. I will make you into a great nation and I will bless you; I will make your name great, and you will be a blessing. I will bless those who bless you, and whoever curses you I will curse; and all people on earth will be blessed through you" (Genesis 12:1–3, NIV).

The promise was overwhelming and required a lot of faith on Abraham's part. He believed God's promises, although he probably didn't understand them fully. Abraham took God at His word and began his journey into the unknown. His faith pleased God, and God promised him a safe journey and reward.

God restated His covenant to Abraham on several different occasions and in many forms. But always, the covenant contained personal promises of blessing for Abraham; the forming of a great nation made up of his descendants; and the possession of the Promised Land of inheritance to Abraham and his descendants.

Abraham was called by God to step out in faith. Just as he was asked to sacrifice his possessions for even greater blessings, God may ask you, too, to make sacrifices. If you are asked to leave the known for the unknown, your obedience will please God.

worth thinking about

- ▶ **God's promised** blessings are always bigger and better than the human mind can imagine. God's covenant promises to Abraham were so great that God explained them to him in stages.

- ▶ **When God blesses** you with His promises, He blesses others through you. God's covenant promises with Abraham rippled outward to bless others.

- ▶ **The covenant** that God made with Abraham was unconditional, meaning that even if Abraham and his descendants had disobeyed God, God would still have kept His promise. The covenant was totally dependent on God's doing what He said He would.

> *It was faith that made Abraham obey when God called him to go out to a country which God had promised to give him. He left his own country without knowing where he was going.*
>
> Hebrews 11:8, GNT

Who are God's children?

It is not the natural children who are God's children, but it is the children of the promise who are regarded as Abraham's offspring.

Romans 9:8, NIV

question

▼

What covenant promise did God give to Moses on Mount Sinai?

Moses was a leader of God's people. You've heard about the parting of the Red Sea, and about how Moses led the people through the wilderness to the Promised Land. You know he received the Ten Commandments from God while on a high mountain, but you'd like to know more. Were the Ten Commandments the covenant promise, or was there more involved? What covenant did God give to Moses? Is it relevant to your life today?

answer

▼

God heard the groaning of His enslaved people. He remembered His unconditional covenant with Abraham and his descendants. Moses was the man God chose to go to the Israelites and free them. Through Moses, God would bring Israel to the Promised Land. A reluctant Moses, along with his brother, Aaron, began their task.

God plagued the land of Egypt until they freed the Israelites. Moses led Israel to worship at the base of Mount Sinai. Moses went to the mountaintop where God gave him the covenant for Israel. The covenant would enable the people to form a nation, and it provided assistance for their journey to the Promised Land. The covenant given to Moses for Israel was conditional. If they obeyed God and kept His covenant, they would be God's chosen people—a priestly kingdom and a holy nation.

The Mosaic covenant included conditions for the journey. If Israel obeyed, God promised an angel of protection and blessings as they traveled to the Promised Land. He would fight their enemies and deliver them. God reminded them of His faithfulness and compassion (Exodus 34:6–7).

When you obey God's laws and principles, you will have peace. God will bless and guide you. He will keep His promises and show you compassion.

worth thinking about

▶ **God's covenant**, given to Moses for the nation of Israel, was the answer to the prayers Israel had uttered back in Egypt.

▶ **Because the covenant** was conditional, God could easily see their hearts. Periods of rebellion made the journey to the Promised Land last forty years. Obedience would have shortened their time in the wilderness.

▶ **The laws** of the covenant were for the good of the people. The imposed conditions were to serve as an encouragement for obedience.

▼

Because the Lord your God is a merciful God, he will neither abandon you nor destroy you; he will not forget the covenant with your ancestors that he swore to them.

Deuteronomy 4:31, NRSV

7

question

▼

What is the covenant promise of love?

People are always saying they *love* this or that, referring to their favorite food, style, or activity. Contemporary society has tossed the word around so lightly that it has lost some of its strength in meaning. You realize that the word *love*, as used in the Bible, has great significance, such as when the Bible says God is love. If that is true, does God make a promise to love? Is there a specific covenant of love?

answer

▼

The entire Bible, inspired by God and written by His chosen people, is a covenant of love. God's love began with the creation of the world. It was evident in the Garden of Eden as He showed forgiveness to Adam and Eve. Every interaction with His chosen people in biblical times is a shout from God, "I love you!"

Any law or promise God made was a covenant of love. When the Israelites were nearing the Promised Land, God reminded them: "If you pay attention to these laws and are careful to follow them, then the LORD your God will keep his covenant of love with you, as he swore to your forefathers" (Deuteronomy 7:12, NIV). Obedience always caused good things—blessings—to surround His people.

God's covenant love is the theme that connects the Old Testament with the New Testament. God's purpose is always to save His people, to bless them with peace, because He loves them and wants to fellowship with them.

When evil entered the world in the Garden of Eden, God knew then that His love would conquer Satan. God's greatest covenant of love was sending His Son into the world to spare the debt of wrongs (the breaking of God's laws), so that all might spend eternity with God in heaven. There is no greater love than when someone will die for you. Every promise that God gives in His Word is His covenant of love to you.

worth thinking about

▶ **God told** the prophet Jeremiah that He knew him before He formed him in the womb for a special work. Likewise, God created you in love and has a plan for your life. He has a covenant of love with you.

▶ **Reading about** the fulfillment of covenant promises shows that God can be trusted. God is not like a fair-weather friend. His love can be counted on.

▶ **Believing a promised** scripture for your life is grabbing hold of God's covenant love.

> *Know therefore that the LORD your God is God;*
> *he is the faithful God, keeping his covenant of*
> *love to a thousand generations of those who*
> *love him and keep his commands.*
> Deuteronomy 7:9, NIV

question

Did God make more than one covenant with the Israelites?

The travels of the Israelites and their journey to the Promised Land is a well-known story. You recognize that the Ten Commandments and other laws were given by God to help govern the nation. God and His chosen people entered into a covenant agreement. You cannot help but think that Israel's journey must have seemed endless, for it lasted forty years. Did the covenant given to them at Mount Sinai cover everything, or did God make other covenants with His people?

answer

The first five books of the Bible—Genesis, Exodus, Leviticus, Numbers, and Deuteronomy—contain God's covenant promises and laws with Abraham and his descendants, who would form the nation of Israel.

When God chose Abraham to be the father of the nation of Israel, He made His first covenant to Abraham and his descendants. God continued to guide and direct Israel by establishing covenants with them through the leaders He chose. God called Moses to free the Israelites and to present His next major covenant for establishing them as a nation. He then expanded it by adding promises and conditions for their journey to the Promised Land.

Throughout biblical history, Israel intended to obey, but was often led astray. During these times, God would always get them back on the path of obedience by speaking through a prophet or a king. The original covenant made with Abraham and his descendants would be renewed and expanded for the good of the people.

God will not break His covenant with you. He is faithful even if you are not. His love will find a way to get you back on track.

worth thinking about

▶ **God will expand** His covenant with you as you grow in your relationship with Him. He will teach you and bless you.

▶ **God never breaks** a covenant; it is not His nature. But mankind's nature is to be easily led astray. The ideal covenant relationship is one in which both parties are faithful to each other. Thankfully, God is forgiving and allows for commitments to be renewed.

▶ **God is patient** with His people. Even if some of His covenants are conditional, His love is unconditional. His love is not based on what you do or do not do.

> The steadfast love of the LORD never ceases,
> his mercies never come to an end; they are
> new every morning; great is your faithfulness.
> "The LORD is my portion," says my soul,
> "therefore I will hope in him!"
> Lamentations 3:22–24, NRSV

9

What covenant promise did God make with King David?

The Bible stories, both good and bad, about King David may be familiar to you. The story of how David killed the giant with a slingshot and pebble may have inspired you to tackle your own giants. David, a shepherd boy who became a king, was far from perfect. He committed adultery with Bathsheba and then had her husband killed. Why would God have made a covenant with someone who made such a mess of his life? Did God make a covenant with David?

answer

Even though David committed adultery with Bathsheba and had her husband murdered, God forgave David. He did discipline him, but God's love for David was unconditional. God loved David even when he failed. He did not discount David's life based on one or two bad things he did. God knew David to the core of his soul. No doubt, God remembered David's faith when he killed Goliath the giant. God loves you with the same kind of unconditional love.

King David loved God and wanted to build a temple for the people to worship in. Up until this time, they had always worshiped in a tent. But God said no, and made an unconditional covenant with David: God promised that kings would always come from David's line, that David's son would succeed him, and that he would be the one to build God's temple. God would discipline David's son if needed, but He would never put an end to His agreement with the son; no one would be allowed to take away the son's kingship; and the throne from David's line would be an everlasting one. David was greatly moved by the promises given in the covenant and offered up a prayer of thanksgiving (2 Samuel 7:12–16, 18–29). God knows your heart, too, and has blessed you with all the wonderful promises in Scripture.

worth thinking about

▶ **The promise** of an everlasting throne was fulfilled when Jesus, God's promised Son and a heavenly King, was born from the lineage of David.

▶ **God's promises** far outweigh any disappointments you may have in this life. David wanted to build God a temple, but when he considered the great promises of the covenant, he was overjoyed by God's goodness.

▶ **David felt unworthy** of such a grand covenant. But he did not let his self-doubt stop him from accepting God's promises with gratefulness.

> *There were fourteen generations from Abraham to David. There were also fourteen from David to the exile in Babylonia and fourteen more to the birth of the Messiah.*
> Matthew 1:17, CEV

question

What is the New Testament covenant promise?

The Bible is divided into two parts, the Old Testament and the New Testament. The Old Testament tells about life before Jesus, and the New Testament begins with His birth. You are wondering if the old laws apply. What difference did the birth of Jesus make? Does it involve more than His birth? Are His death and resurrection factors? Why do people refer to the New Testament as a new covenant?

answer

The Israelites, God's chosen people, lived under the covenant of the Law. They soon learned that the Old Testament laws were impossible to keep. Try as they might, they always needed to atone—to make amends— for their wrongs. They understood that the penalty for breaking God's law was death. Offerings or sacrifices of animals were allowed for sins committed in ignorance. But no matter how hard they worked to be obedient, they always ended up failing. Imagine the fear and guilt they continually carried in their hearts and minds.

When Jesus was born, the angels heralded His arrival as the Savior—One who would deliver God's people from the punishment they deserved. Jesus' death and resurrection established the new covenant. Jesus spoke of it at the last Passover meal He shared with His disciples. "This cup that is poured out for you is the new covenant in my blood" (Luke 22:20, NRSV). Jesus went to the cross and died in your place. He gave you the free gift of grace—undeserved favor. The new covenant is the covenant of grace. You are free from the law.

The new covenant is good news! "The wages of sin is death, but the free gift of God is eternal life in Christ Jesus our Lord" (Romans 6:23, NRSV).

worth thinking about

- ▶ **The Bible teaches** that everyone is in need of His grace. When you accept God's gift, you are justified by what Jesus did on your behalf. It is just as if you never sinned.

- ▶ **Love for Jesus** and thankfulness for His free gift will cause you to try to obey God's laws. You will still have times when you fall short, but you will have an overwhelming desire to please God.

- ▶ **The new covenant** is available to all people on earth. It is for *everyone* who believes in Jesus.

> For this reason Christ is the one who arranges a new covenant, so that those who have been called by God may receive the eternal blessings that God has promised. This can be done because there has been a death which sets people free from the wrongs they did while the first covenant was in effect.
>
> Hebrews 9:15, GNT

11 question

How are you God's promise?

Everyone is striving for perfection in today's crazy world. It screams at you from the ads: get the perfect body, the perfect house, the perfect car, the perfect job, and then you will be accepted. When people fail to measure up, they experience put-downs from themselves or from others. Where can people find their value? Does anyone look beyond the exterior and see what's inside? How does God see you? Does He see your potential and value?

answer

God the Creator delighted in making you special. You gave Him joy and still do. The Book of Genesis says that when God viewed His created work, He declared it was good. When God looks at you, He declares that you are good. God values you because He created you in His image. But no one is perfect except God. Designers and society may say if you look like this, or own that particular style, you will reach perfection, but that is an opinion and a lie.

God makes each person unique. He may have given you a winning smile, or some other special personality trait. He grants to each person abilities and talents that enable him or her to contribute to the good of mankind. God never intended the world to be made up of carbon-copy people.

When God looks at you, He sees all the possibilities He placed within you when He formed you in your mother's womb. "You are the one who put me together inside my mother's body, and I praise you because of the wonderful way you created me" (Psalm 139:13–14, CEV). He sees who you are and who you can be when you choose to live a life that is pleasing to Him. He sees you as a promise with the potential to be all He created you to be.

worth thinking about

▶ **God looks** at you and sees the promise of a close relationship with Him. Because you are made in His image, you share similar thoughts and feelings. You can share all your concerns with Him.

▶ **God looks** at you and sees the promise that you can be His legs and arms on earth. When you try to please God, your interests and purposes will line up with His.

▶ **God looks** at you and sees the promise of your future. He has a grand design for your life, and He will guide you in discovering its path.

> The LORD gave me this message: "I knew you before I formed you in your mother's womb. Before you were born I set you apart and appointed you as my prophet to the nations.
> Jeremiah 1:4–5, NLT

12

question

How does God promise to love you?

People are always telling you that God is love, but no one ever explains what that means. Does God love you in general, the way He loves all the people in the world? Does He love you specifically, caring about your individual needs? You've always figured that He loves you when you're being kind and thoughtful. But what about those times when you're being a pain? You wish that someone would explain exactly *how* God loves you.

answer

God loves you unconditionally. His love is not dependent on your behavior. He has a promise just for you. "When the fullness of time had come, God sent his Son, born of a woman, born under the law, in order to redeem those who were under the law, so that we might receive adoption as children" (Galatians 4:4–5, NRSV). The passage goes on to say that your heart cries out, *Abba*, which is the Aramaic word for *father*. The word implies a close relationship, like a daddy's relationship to his child. By this, you can understand that God loves each person individually.

God loves you *abundantly*. He delights in giving you good things. "It is just as the Scriptures say, 'What God has planned for people who love him is more than eyes have seen or ears have heard. It has never even entered our minds!'" (1 Corinthians 2:9, CEV).

God loves you *enduringly*. God's love will not wear thin. He never gets tired of you. The writer of Psalm 136 said over and over that God's love endures, that it will never stop.

God loves you *completely*. "We can understand someone dying for a person worth dying for, and we can understand how someone good and noble could inspire us to selfless sacrifice. But God put his love on the line for us by offering his Son in sacrificial death while we were of no use whatever to him" (Romans 5:7–8, THE MESSAGE).

worth thinking about

▶ **God's love makes** you rich. You are rich because He is kind to you, not treating you as you deserve. You are rich because He gives you good things.

▶ **God's love cannot** be measured. When you consider the vastness of the ocean or the universe, you get a glimmer of God's infinite love.

▶ **God's love fills** your inner being. The Bible says that Jesus is the *Living Water* and the *Bread of Life*, satisfying that gnawing hunger in your spirit.

> The LORD your God wins victory after victory and is always with you. He celebrates and sings because of you, and he will refresh your life with his love.
> Zephaniah 3:17, CEV

13

question
▼
What promise does God have for your life?

It is a pivotal point in time. You have decisions to make in your life. You know the choice you make will have long-range effects, not only on you but also on others. You feel like the traveler in Robert Frost's "The Road Not Taken." You're standing at the fork in the road, and you have to choose. How can you know for sure what you should do? You'd like to know, does God have a plan for your life?

answer
▼

Before you were conceived and formed in your mother's womb, you were a thought in God's mind. He created you with purpose, and gave you unique talents and gifts. Jeremiah was a prophet who lived in biblical times. One day God spoke to him directly: "Surely I know the plans I have for you, says the LORD, plans for your welfare and not for harm, to give you a future with hope" (Jeremiah 29:11, NRSV). These words recorded in the Bible are relevant to you and your search: God has a plan for your life. It is a good plan that is going to fill your life with purpose. You will benefit from it and not be harmed.

There is great comfort in that assurance, but what if you're still confused over which path to take? Long ago,

God spoke to another prophet named Isaiah. God told him to tell the people who lived in Jerusalem, "Your teacher will be right there, local and on the job, urging you on whenever you wander left or right: 'This is the right road. Walk down this road'" (Isaiah 30:20–21, THE MESSAGE). Even if you start down the road that will be a dead end for you, God will nudge you in the right direction through prayer and the feeling of calm He puts in your heart. He may turn you around by the circumstances that He places in your life. He may place a special verse from the Bible right in front of you, and you'll feel that He is speaking directly to you through His written word. As God told Isaiah, He will get your attention.

worth thinking about

▶ **Bumpy roads** occur in every life. Even with God as your teacher, there will be some rough sections of road. The bumps will not destroy you; they will form your character. God will be at your side, guiding you toward His purpose for your life.

▶ **Detours are** confusing, but they often have to do with God's perfect timing. He will put you in the right place at the right time.

▶ **The Bible is** God's road map for your life. He has given you unique talents and skills. Skills, along with what you enjoy, are signs pointing to your purpose.

> The LORD says, "I will guide you along the best pathway for your life. I will advise you and watch over you."
> Psalm 32:8, NLT

14

question

Does God promise to forgive all wrongs?

On the evening news, the late-breaking story was about a convicted serial killer who learned about God while imprisoned. Although this convict had learned about God, that fact did not do away with the fact that he had killed many people. Will God forget all his crimes? Will God allow a murderer to go to heaven as if he had done nothing wrong? Isn't God supposed to be a fair judge? Does He really forgive all wrongdoing?

answer

Ask the average man on the street whether one wrong is worse than another, and most assuredly, he will tell you yes. But God has a different answer. Some men in authority once brought a woman caught in the act of adultery to Jesus. The custom at that time was to stone her. However, Jesus did not condemn her; rather, He said, "Let anyone among you who is without sin be the first to throw a stone at her" (John 8:7, NRSV). One by one the boisterous mob left. Jesus did not regard her act as greater than the accusations and anger exhibited by the crowd.

James, the brother of Christ, explained it more fully in his book of the Bible, "Whoever keeps the whole law but fails in one point has become accountable for all of it" (James 2:10, NRSV).

God does not give a list of wrongs that cannot be erased by Jesus' death and resurrection. But He does promise that because He died for you, your wrongdoing can be forgiven and swept away. All your mess-ups—past, present, and future—were forgiven on the day Jesus died. When you know Jesus, God no longer sees what you have done wrong.

worth thinking about

- ▶ **Comparing yourself** to others will leave you frustrated. Someone will always be better or worse.

- ▶ **Some people think** they would never be involved in a major wrong, but a proverb in the Bible says, "First pride, then the crash—the bigger the ego, the harder the fall" (Proverbs 16:18, THE MESSAGE).

- ▶ **It is good** to be aware of the Old Testament laws and understand what actions displease God. But when Jesus came, He did not come to condemn the world, but to save it by God's gift of grace—undeserved favor—which covers all wrongs.

> *We are made right with God by placing our faith in Jesus Christ. And this is true for everyone who believes, no matter who we are.*
>
> Romans 3:22, NLT

question

▼

Does God promise happiness?

Some people think it is possible to have God's joy in tough times. But that does not make sense to you. After all, people are truly happy when things are going their way and there are no problems. Are joy and happiness different? Why doesn't God continually surround His people with happy circumstances? Since bad things do happen to good people, you have to question, does God care about personal happiness? What does the Bible say about the promise of happiness?

answer

▼

There is nothing wrong with being happy. Life is for celebrating the good times that come your way. But the happiness that a special occasion or a gift provides soon fades into a good memory. A look at society today reveals that events and purchases have to keep getting bigger and better in order for people to maintain their mountaintop experience.

Happiness and joy are different. Happiness is a party. It is receiving a special gift or making a long-awaited purchase. Joy could be called a long-lasting type of happiness, but it is more like a peace within your heart. Joy is the result of trusting God in difficult circumstances. God knows that

His people need both happy and difficult times. The good times are for celebrating, and the trying times are for developing character.

A glance at the biblical story of Joseph reveals God at work. Joseph's entire life was filled with unhappy circumstances. There was little to celebrate. He was sold as a slave by his half brothers, accused falsely, and imprisoned. Joseph could not have been happy during these troubling years. But God was more interested in the development of Joseph's character than in Joseph's personal happiness. Joseph did experience inner peace and joy because he trusted God. God works the same way in your life. He knows that trials shape you to be all that you can be.

worth thinking about

▶ **God allows** smooth terrain in your life, but He also trains you to stay in the race by persevering through trials.

▶ **Character-building** exercise produces inner joy in the same way that weight training produces physical muscle. God knows everyone must have spiritual workouts.

▶ **Happy times** happen to you, but joy is happiness within you. God is more concerned with life-endurance training, which produces joy that continues in all circumstances.

> *I will be glad and rejoice in your unfailing love, for you have seen my troubles, and you care about the anguish of my soul.*
> Psalm 31:7, NLT

Why did the Son of God come?

We know that the Son of God came so we could recognize and understand the truth of God—what a gift!—and we are living in the Truth itself, in God's Son, Jesus Christ. This Jesus is both True God and Real Life.

1 John 5:20, THE MESSAGE

16 question

Do God's promises cover the little things in your life?

A friend shared that she often prays for God to help her find specific items or bargains when shopping. She believes that He does. Another friend insists that God favors her with good parking places. There are serious needs in this world. Why would God bother with small things? You'd really like to know. Is God concerned about the little things in your life?

answer

The Bible says, "What is the price of two sparrows—one copper coin? But not a single sparrow can fall to the ground without your Father knowing it. And the very hairs on your head are all numbered" (Matthew 10:29–30, NLT). A woman who makes a quilt is concerned with the placement of every stitch and with the care of the quilt after it is finished. A man who builds a house is aware of the placement of every nail and with the upkeep of the home after it is built. Likewise, God is aware of every detail of your life and cares for all your needs.

Finite minds cannot even begin to comprehend the magnitude of God's power to do all things, to be all places, and to be all-knowing. And yet the Bible explains that He possesses all these qualities. If you think God does not care about the little things in your life, you place Him in a box and limit His powers.

God loves to give good gifts to His children. "God saved you by his grace when you believed. And you can't take credit for this; it is a gift from God" (Ephesians 2:8, NLT). This was His supreme gift to you, but He also delights in giving in many other ways, both large and small. He enjoys seeing a smile on your face and a spring in your step.

worth thinking about

▶ **Think of** the gifts you give to those you love. Some are costly and some are small tokens, but they delight the recipient. Why would God not give both types of gifts?

▶ **In order to** give a desired gift to a loved one, you need to know what he or she wants. Prayer is sharing the desires of your heart, as well as your needs.

▶ **"The LORD guides** us in the way we should go and protects those who please him" (Psalm 37:23, GNT). This implies that nothing happens by chance in a believer's life. The daily delights along the way are all gifts from God.

> *As bad as you are, you know how to give good things to your children. How much more, then, will your Father in heaven give good things to those who ask him!*
> Matthew 7:11, GNT

17 question

How does God promise to supply your needs?

Everyone keeps telling you that God will take care of you and supply your needs. But you do not know how they can be so sure. Your needs are multiple, and you've never been one to leave things up to chance. You like to be in control. It is easy for people to spout platitudes about trusting God. But you want to know the *how* before you hand over the remote of your life. How does God supply a person's mental, physical, and spiritual needs?

answer

This question revolves around a trust issue. God's Son, Jesus, spoke these words: "If God gives such attention to the wildflowers, most of them never even seen, don't you think he'll attend to you, take pride in you, do his best for you? What I'm trying to do here is get you to relax, not be so preoccupied with *getting* so you can respond to God's *giving*. People who don't know God and the way he works fuss over these things, but you know both God and how he works" (Luke 12:28–30, THE MESSAGE). All your needs will be supplied by God when you seek Him. God will favor you by providing the means for your daily necessities.

Also, you might never be rich in the world's eyes, but you will certainly be rich in God's eyes. Paul, a biblical writer and one of God's devoted workers, wrote this assurance to his friends: "This same God who takes care of me will supply all your needs from his glorious riches, which have been given to us in Christ Jesus" (Philippians 4:19, NLT).

In addition, God will protect your mental and emotional outlook. "Do not worry about anything, but in everything by prayer and supplication with thanksgiving, let your requests be made known to God. And the peace of God, which surpasses all understanding, will guard your hearts and your minds in Christ Jesus" (Philippians 4:6–7, NRSV). Whatever your need, God has you covered.

worth thinking about

▶ **Needs and wants** are two different things. God sent manna (a bread-like substance) and quail to the Israelites in the wilderness. He supplied their need, but they wanted more. God supplies your need, but you may not be satisfied.

▶ **When taking** inventory of what God has given to you, whether physically visible or sensed in your spirit, being grateful will rid your mind and heart of anxiety.

▶ **The riches** given by God's Spirit can never be gambled away or lost in an investment. They will last indefinitely.

> *I once was young, now I'm a graybeard—not once have I seen an abandoned believer, or his kids out roaming the streets.*
> Psalm 37:25, THE MESSAGE

18 question

Does God promise to always love you?

Have you ever been so grouchy and mean-spirited that you felt unlovable? Not only do you not like others when you're acting ugly, but you also do not like yourself. You try to stay out of everyone's way for fear you'll snap. You know yourself; you may say or do something you'll regret. You wonder how God can love you. Will He get fed up and turn aside when you act like a wretch? Will He get mad enough to stop loving you?

answer

Imagine yourself as a parent who loves your child deeply. One day the child does something you do not like. In fact, the child breaks your heart. You may be at the point of tears or even furious, but you do not stop loving your child.

The Bible refers to God as your heavenly Father. Think about your reactions as a parent, and you will have a better understanding of God's love toward you. True, the six o'clock news makes you aware that not all parents care about their children, but this is not true of God. Paul, an early Christian writer, quoted a promise of God in the Scriptures: "Never will I leave you; never will I forsake you" (Hebrews 13:5, NIV). God will not desert you. His love is not based on what you do or do not do. You cannot make God stop loving you or turn away from you.

How can you know this is how God operates? The Bible is filled with stories about men and women who made big-time mistakes or wanted to do things their way: Moses, who was a reluctant leader; Jacob, who lied to his father; King David, who committed murder and adultery; and the list goes on. These people all died loved by God. No doubt their stories are included to assure you that God is love and that His love knows no end.

worth thinking about

▶ **You may refer** to someone as a teacher, a doctor, a nurse, or an engineer—that's the thing a person does. Scripture tells you that God is love. Love cannot stop loving.

▶ **God says** if you tell Him when you've done wrong, He will remove the wrong and let you start over. Only a loving God would find a way to wipe your slate clean.

▶ **God created** the world and everything in it, including humanity. God saw His creation and was pleased. Because God is your Creator, He understands your humanness.

> Such love has no fear, because perfect love expels all fear. If we are afraid, it is for fear of punishment, and this shows that we have not fully experienced his perfect love.
>
> 1 John 4:18, NLT

question

Does God promise to keep you safe?

Life is just one big risk-taking adventure. Accidents may happen whether you are driving a car or flying a plane. If you dwell on it, you'll be afraid to venture anywhere. Even staying in is no guarantee of safety. All kinds of dangers lurk in the home. You hear about these dangers on the evening news, and it is unnerving. How can you relax and let go of your anxiety? Does God promise to keep you safe?

answer

One of the ways God keeps His people safe is by surrounding them with His ministering angels. Psalm 91 says that when you depend on the Lord, He will order His angels to protect you. Corrie ten Boom, a devout woman who spent time in a Nazi concentration camp, told how she carried her Bible under her dress while passing through inspection. She prayed for angels to surround her, and it seemed to her that she was almost invisible. Corrie was in a frightening situation, but she never lost sight of the fact that God would be her protector.

God's angels are watching over you no matter where you are or what you are doing. You can trust that God has His eye on you, for Psalm 121 says He never slumbers or sleeps. You can relax and let your fears evaporate when you trust God to watch over you.

God provides other spiritual means of protection to His people. God's Holy Spirit lives within you to provide guidance. Another means of protection is prayer. Prayer is a fast and easy way to communicate with God. Call upon God when your need for protection is great, and He promises to answer. The Bible says that even calling out God's name will protect you. In addition, the Bible is filled with many laws and principles that will keep you safe when you obey them. The pages of the Bible are filled with wisdom. You can rest easy, for God has you covered.

worth thinking about

▶ **Trust your God** and not your feelings of fear. Believing in God's promises of protection will cause your fear to melt away.

▶ **The question** of why bad things happen to good people always surfaces in discussions about God keeping mankind safe. Perhaps God is testing someone. A person may be in a vulnerable situation. Maybe someone's time on earth has run out, for "there is a time for birth and death" (Ecclesiastes 3:2, CEV).

▶ **God is in control.** Psalm 11 says God knows and sees all. Nothing happens without His permission. He will bring good from whatever happens.

> *The LORD will protect you from all danger;*
> *he will keep you safe. He will protect you*
> *as you come and go now and forever.*
> Psalm 121:7–8, GNT

question

▾

Can you trust God to keep His promises?

Sometimes you've promised to do this or that for someone, but it did not happen. You meant for it to, but you lacked follow-through, or you just plain ran out of time. Personally, you have been betrayed more times then you want to admit, some times worse than others. How can you be sure that God will keep His promises? A lot of people are in the world, and who are you that God would faithfully keep His word to you?

answer

▾

God will keep His word to you because He esteems you as His created. He holds you in such high regard that He sent His Son, Jesus, to deliver you from the world's evil. Scripture says, "He celebrates and sings because of you, and he will refresh your life with his love" (Zephaniah 3:17, CEV).

God is perfect, without fault, while humans are prone to do wrong. God's relationship with His people can be likened to a marriage where one partner is unfaithful and the other is faithful. Mankind is the unfaithful partner, while God is the faithful one. You can be assured of His faithfulness, for the Bible says that God never breaks a promise. "God has given us both his promise and his oath. These two things are unchangeable because it is impossible for God to lie. Therefore, we who have fled to him for refuge can have great confidence as we hold to the hope that lies before us" (Hebrews 6:18, NLT).

Another example of God's faithfulness is evidenced in His fulfilled prophecies. A biblical prophecy is the foretelling of the future by God and the speaking of it to His people through the prophets. The list of prophecies that have been fulfilled is lengthy. What better proof could there be that God keeps His promises? He will not fail you!

worth thinking about

▶ **It pays to take** God at His word. God warned Noah about the Flood. If Noah had not believed and built the ark, he and his family would have been destroyed.

▶ **Trust grows** when you know the Bible. God foretold that His Son would be born of a virgin and would help His people. Joseph and Mary knew God's prophecies and believed His promises concerning the Babe.

▶ **Recognize your worth** in God's eyes. He treasures His relationship with you and will keep His promises. "I will not forget you! See, I have engraved you on the palms of my hands" (Isaiah 49:15–16, NIV).

▼

Understand, therefore, that the LORD *your God is indeed God. He is the faithful God who keeps his covenant for a thousand generations and lavishes his unfailing love on those who love him and obey his commands.*

Deuteronomy 7:9, NLT

question

Does God promise to restore you?

Bad things happen to good people, and their lives are forever changed. One minute they are ordinary people living ordinary lives, then tragedy strikes, and they are never the same. Endlessly, they go over the circumstances and try to make sense of what happened to them. Will God help them escape their tragic memories? Will He move them past the low place in their lives and restore them? Does God promise restoration to His people?

answer

God is a God of restoration. "I will give you back what you lost in the years when swarms of locusts ate your crops" (Joel 2:25, GNT). Although this was written to the people of Judah when their crops had been devastated, it is relevant to anyone who has suffered loss. God can restore, and He does restore.

God wants you to look to the future. "Do not cling to events of the past or dwell on what happened long ago" (Isaiah 43:18, GNT). God knows that the finger of history writes with permanent ink. No amount of thinking can change what has happened. Your healing will be in looking to the future. In time, God will enable you to use your pain to reach out to others who have suffered similar circumstances. God will use you and your pain to bring hope to others.

God saw what happened to you, and He felt your pain. He will bring healing to you. Hold tight to His hand as He brings you through the restoration process. It may not happen overnight, but it will happen. God will dim the bad memories. You may never forget them, but He will take away their ability to hurt you. He will give you strength to move forward in your life. You will be able to say with the psalmist, "He restores my soul" (Psalm 23:3, NIV).

worth thinking about

▶ Be patient with yourself. God created your body and mind with the ability to heal. Remember, physical wounds do not heal overnight and neither do emotional wounds. Scarring may occur, but the pain goes away.

▶ Be kind to yourself. God loves you and does not want you to suffer mental anguish. "When you call on me, when you come and pray to me, I'll listen" (Jeremiah 29:12, The Message). He will heal your damaged emotions.

▶ Be forgiving of whoever hurt you. It seems impossible, but God will deal with them. When you choose forgiveness, you choose emotional freedom.

> He won't break off a bent reed or put
> out a dying flame, but he will make
> sure that justice is done.
> Isaiah 42:3, CEV

▼

Does God promise to provide when you've lost everything?

Everything—all of your possessions, important papers, and photographs—was wiped out by nature's fury. Shocked by the suddenness, you can hardly take it in. All the material things you valued are gone. Happily, you and your family are safe. Others around you have not been as fortunate. Now you have no choice but to begin anew. But the question is how. Will God help you? Does He promise to provide when you've lost everything? What does the Bible say?

answer

▼

Suffering caused by a disaster can occur to anyone. Until the end of life as we know it, good and evil live side by side. Jesus said, referring to God the Father, "He makes his sun to shine on bad and good people alike, and gives rain to those who do good and to those who do evil" (Matthew 5:45, GNT).

Human nature seeks to understand the *why* of a disaster. The questions pepper our thoughts: Is God punishing you? Are you being tested? Were you careless? A man named Job, who lived in biblical times and suffered disasters, came to a conclusion. Job discovered that it is impossible for human minds to comprehend God's reasons, for they all are part of a bigger picture. Job chose to trust God, and he learned that God does provide. "The LORD made Job twice as rich as he had been before" (Job 42:10, CEV).

The Book of 2 Kings and the Book of 2 Chronicles tell of a national disaster that occurred. The Babylonians attacked the city of Jerusalem. They burned the temple, looted, and broke down the city walls. The city's survivors were forced into exile for seventy years. The people had lost everything, but God supplied their daily needs. God is still providing today. God moves people's hearts to give of their time, money, and possessions to help those in need. He always cares for His own.

worth thinking about

- ▶ **Job did not** play the blame game. "In spite of everything, Job did not sin or accuse God of doing wrong" (Job 1:22, CEV).

- ▶ **Get ready** to be blessed. God will provide by sending help through His people. God's people work together to build one another up physically, spiritually, and emotionally.

- ▶ **Look to the future**, for God will provide. Focus on the new life you will have. God will walk with you through your pain of loss and heal you.

> *Be merciful to me, O God, be merciful, because I come to you for safety. In the shadow of your wings I find protection until the raging storms are over.*
>
> Psalm 57:1, GNT

23

Will God's promises help with illness?

The doctor has just told you that you have cancer, a life-threatening disease. Your mind fires a million questions as you try to comprehend what this means to your life: Will you survive? What surgeries and treatments will be involved? Will you lose your hair and be sick? Will you be able to work? If not, how will you manage financially? Then, of all the questions, there are the biggies: Why? Why is this happening to you? Will God help you in this hour of need?

answer

When Jesus lived on earth, He walked about preaching and healing the sick. Today, God uses the field of medicine to bring healing. Every day, you hear of medical advances. Short of having lived when Jesus walked the earth, you are living in the best possible time to beat any type of disease, including cancer.

Prayer can bring healing, too. "Are any among you sick? They should send for the church elders, who will pray for them and rub olive oil on them in the name of the Lord" (James 5:14, GNT). Believing and knowing that God uses modern medicine and prayer will give you courage.

But God promises even more. He's going to go through

it with you. "Do not be afraid, for I have ransomed you. I have called you by name; you are mine. When you go through deep waters, I will be with you. When you go through rivers of difficulty, you will not drown. When you walk through the fire of oppression, you will not be burned up; the flames will not consume you. For I am the Lord, your God, the Holy One of Israel, your Savior." (Isaiah 43:1–3, NLT).

God offers a daily prescription of peace through the Book of Psalms. The soothing words of the psalmist will bring healing to your spirit, which transfers to your physical body. "Even if I go through the deepest darkness, I will not be afraid" (Psalm 23:4, GNT).

worth thinking about

▶ **God is the friend** who is always with you. He is there when you are sleeping or awake.

▶ **God is the counselor** who keeps you sane and helps you make decisions about what cancer center to go to, which doctor to trust, and what treatment to have. Talk to Him in prayer, and listen for Him to speak in your mind or through circumstances.

▶ **God is your fear-carrier.** Give your fears to Him daily: the fear that His plan may not be the same as yours, and the fears you have about your family.

Heal me, O LORD, and I shall be healed; save me, and I shall be saved; for you are my praise.
Jeremiah 17:14, NRSV

question

▼

Does God promise to relieve you of guilt?

Guilt is something that many people carry around with them every day. They cannot seem to feel God's forgiveness. Maybe they will not accept it, or perhaps they will not forgive themselves. Whatever the reason, they end up living defeated lives, always feeling unworthy. Sometimes they claim guilt when it is plain to see they are not the guilty party. Can God free them from their excess guilt? Does He promise to set them free?

answer

▼

There are many reasons that people feel guilty. Sometimes it is because they really are. They may have committed wrongs that they have not confessed to God. King David spoke of how guilt affects you. "Before I confessed my sins, my bones felt limp, and I groaned all day long" (Psalm 32:3, CEV). David was as weighted down as if he had been carrying a big bag of rocks on his back. "So I confessed my sins and told them all to you. I said, 'I'll tell the LORD each one of my sins.' Then you forgave me and took away my guilt" (Psalm 32:5, CEV). David's guilt was relieved when he confessed, because God took it away.

God is still relieving guilt today through His gift of grace. The gift of undeserved favor was made available when

Jesus died and paid the debt for everyone's wrong actions. Accepting the gift of grace, and believing it was for you personally, erases your guilt. You may need to take another step and forgive yourself.

But sometimes, things have happened to people that make them feel shame. These people learn to feel guilty and to accept other people's guilt. This is called false guilt. God will relieve false guilt when they choose to believe the truth of the Bible—they are forgiven. God's purpose has always been to relieve His people from their guilt. He does this through Jesus and the truth of His Word.

worth thinking about

▶ **God forgives**, and you can, too. Forgiveness is a choice, so choose to forgive yourself and anyone who tries to blame you for their mistakes.

▶ **Through prayer** and the study of the Scriptures, you can learn to cast off false guilt and move on to healthier thinking. Jesus promised that the truth found in the Scriptures will set you free.

▶ **Feelings of unworthiness** and shame are not from God. Satan nags at people by reminding them of past failures. He keeps them paralyzed with guilt. Jesus took your guilt, and you are free to move on.

> *If we confess our sins to God, he will keep his promise and do what is right: he will forgive us our sins and purify us from all our wrongdoing.*
>
> 1 John 1:9, GNT

25 question

Does God promise never to forsake you?

False accusations have been brought against you. When the situation first came up you were not worried, for you thought the truth would win out. Now you're not so sure. What if you cannot prove the accusations are false? You're even questioning whether your family and friends believe you. Many people tend to believe the worst. Maybe you're becoming paranoid. Will God help you when you've been accused unfairly? Does He promise never to forsake you?

answer

The Book of Hebrews promises that God will never forsake you or leave you. Cling to that promise, and let it be your anchor during this time of trial. You have the power of God on your side. "We can say with confidence, 'The Lord is my helper; I will not be afraid. What can anyone do to me?'" (Hebrews 13:6, NRSV). God never forgets His own. He loves justice, and He loves you.

Jesus understands how you are suffering, for He, too, was accused falsely. Let God deal with those who are hurling accusations. He will bring to light the true motive of their hearts.

Trust God to work behind the scenes on your behalf. It is affirming if your family and friends believe in you, but the most important thing is that God knows your heart.

Even if you are judged wrongly, God will not cease to work on clearing your name. Joseph, a biblical character of old, was accused unfairly and imprisoned. The good news came later, when God had him freed and gave him a prominent position and family. Whatever happens, God will go through this time of trouble with you. He will not turn away from you when you ask Him to help you with this situation. You can count on His love and protection. He is on your side.

worth thinking about

▶ **Jesus understands** what it is like to have your family doubt you. His family did not understand His refusal to quit preaching. "They thought he was crazy" (Mark 3:21, CEV).

▶ **God is a** fair judge who demands justice. "The LORD loves what is right and does not abandon his faithful people. He protects them forever" (Psalm 37:28, GNT).

▶ **Paul and Silas,** the Lord's workers, were accused falsely and jailed. Still, they thanked God and sang of His love. God saw that they were set free.

My protector is nearby; no one can stand here to accuse me of wrong. The LORD God will help me and prove I am innocent. My accusers will wear out like moth-eaten clothes.

Isaiah 50:8–9, CEV

What hope is there in troubled times?

Why are you downcast, O my soul? Why so disturbed within me? Put your hope in God, for I will yet praise him, my Savior and my God.

Psalm 42:5, NIV

question

How do God's promises help you face financial problems?

Finances are sometimes difficult to juggle in this day and age. Credit cards make buying too tempting for those who are prone to buy on impulse. But even the most conscientious shopper is often left trying to balance the books at the end of the month, if they've given in to the buy-now-pay-later lifestyle. Does God care about financial woes? If you ask, will He help you? Does God give specific promises of help?

answer

When money is tight you tend to worry. You cannot see any way to trim your budget, or even think of a way to increase your income. Whatever the cause of the money crunch, God does not want you to drown in anxiety. The Bible says that God promises to provide.

Every material blessing is a gift from God. He desires that you be a good steward, a caretaker, of what He has entrusted to you. When you share what He has given you with God's people or those in need, it is as if you are giving back to God. When you give, God blesses your finances and provides a way for your needs to be taken care of. If you need a helping hand, He will send people to help you. If you need a job, He will provide a job opportunity, for God does expect you to work and pay your bills. "Work and you will earn a living; if you sit around talking you will be poor" (Proverbs 14:23, GNT). If bills and income do not match up, one of two things will be necessary: a lifestyle change, or finding a job that pays more. Either way, God will give you direction when you talk to Him in prayer. Give God the worry, and seek His counsel on dealing with your financial problems. You can trust God's promise to supply your need. He will teach you how to deal with your finances wisely.

worth thinking about

▶ **Jesus told** His followers to look at how God takes care of nature—the birds of the air and the wildflowers. He said not to question God's provision, just to trust His promise.

▶ **Stirring up** a sharing heart for God always rewards a generous giver. "The measure you use for others is the one that God will use for you" (Luke 6:38, GNT). We always have something that someone else can use.

▶ **Paul, God's worker,** had times of plenty and times of need. He learned to be content whatever his situation, for His hope and trust were in God.

"Bring all the tithes into the storehouse so there will be enough food in my Temple. If you do," says the LORD of Heaven's Armies, "I will open the windows of heaven for you. I will pour out a blessing so great you won't have enough room to take it in!"
Malachi 3:10, NLT

question

What are God's promises for freeing you from addiction?

Addictions sneak up on people when least expected and wrap their tentacles around them, making them feel powerless to escape. They can destroy a life, an entire family, or even more. Psychologists argue that some people have addictive personalities and become easily entangled. But the truth is that most of mankind has encountered some type of overpowering addiction. Can God help people who are ensnared by an addiction? Does He promise to help free those who are struggling?

answer

Addictive behaviors come in all shapes and sizes; some are major and some are minor. Some destroy your life instantly, and others over time. But God is the answer for whatever type of addiction you are battling. "You were told that your foolish desires will destroy you and that you must give up your old way of life with all its bad habits. Let the Spirit change your way of thinking and make you into a new person" (Ephesians 4:22–24, CEV). Jesus asked a paralyzed man, who had lain by a healing pool for thirty-eight years, if he really wanted to get well. The man explained that when the angel stirred the water, he had no one to help him in. Those who are entrapped by an addiction need to ask themselves the question Jesus asked. Do you really want to get well?

If the answer is yes, help is available. God will help you win in your spirit and in your physical body. God uses people, and there are many medical and counseling services available to help with recovery from an addiction. Remember the greatness of God's power. "This power working in us is the same as the mighty strength which he used when he raised Christ from death and seated him at his right side in the heavenly world" (Ephesians 1:19–20, GNT). God's power, which defeated death, is available to defeat your addiction. You're bound to be a winner with God.

worth thinking about

▶ **God is your** strength. When you are weak, God promises to be strong in you. He is the mortar to your bricks and will hold you firmly in place.

▶ **God's Son**, Jesus, is like a vine. You are like a branch. Staying attached to the Vine will allow you to draw nourishment. His nourishment provides the power to overcome.

▶ **Psalm 23 promises** that God restores your soul. When you reach out to Him for deliverance, He will change and restore you.

> *Death attacked from all sides, and I was captured by its painful chains. But when I was really hurting, I prayed and said, "LORD, please don't let me die!"*
> Psalm 116:3–4, CEV

question

▼

Does God promise to help you bear your grief?

Life goes right on while you are wrapped in a cocoon of pain. Some people do not even notice, while others do but stand helplessly watching. When someone asks how you are, you say fine, but your heart cries: *My life has just been splintered into a thousand pieces, and I'll never be all right again.* Will it ever change, or are you destined to live out the rest of your days in this numbness of soul? Can God help you bear your grief?

answer

▼

"The LORD is close to the brokenhearted and saves those who are crushed in spirit" (Psalm 34:18, NIV). He knows the loss of a loved one breaks your heart. Even Jesus wept when His friend Lazarus died. God is in heaven and has a panoramic view of centuries of time. The reason behind the timing of events is beyond our understanding, but God knows the why. Peace will come to you when you trust that God knows best. "The LORD is my strength and my shield; my heart trusts in him, and I am helped" (Psalm 28:7, NIV).

God is a comforter. He comforts you by sending other people to help you. He comforts you by sending touching sentiments that have meaning only to you—a ray of sunshine, a light bathing a dark hillside, or a bird singing. He comforts you through His Scriptures. "Do not let your hearts be troubled. Trust in God; trust also in me. In my Father's house are many rooms; if it were not so, I would have told you. I am going there to prepare a place for you" (John 14:1–2, NIV). The good news, the comforting news, is that life is not over when you die a physical death. Eternity stretches before you, and it is possible to spend forever with Him and be reunited with your loved ones.

worth thinking about

▶ **God is like** a daddy who will hold your hand in the dark. "Weeping may linger for the night, but joy comes with the morning" (Psalm 30:5, NRSV).

▶ **God is like** a doctor who applies an ointment to your wounds. In the land of Gilead they made a balm from the gum of native trees, which was used for physical pain. God's comfort is like the balm of Gilead and heals our broken heart.

▶ **Jesus is the** Shepherd who will lead you from the valley of sorrow. He will guide you to the opening that is called the door of hope.

> *Jesus said to her, "I am the resurrection and the life. He who believes in me will live, even though he dies."*
> John 11:25, NIV

29

question

▼

Does God promise to lift your depression?

Depression squeezes the meaning from life and leaves its recipient with an overwhelming sense of sadness. Life is colorless for its victims. Every step is an effort for those who are battling depression. Nights spent tossing and turning rob them of their daily energy. Concentration is impossible, and every molehill is a mountain. Can God help them out of this pit they are in? Does He care about their struggle? What are God's promises for overcoming depression?

answer

▼

God created you with three aspects: physical, emotional, and spiritual. God gives you work and rest to take care of the physical. He gives you purpose and relationships to engage your emotions, and He calls you to Him for your spiritual nurturing. When you neglect or encounter problems within any one of the three areas, depression may hit and cause you to spiral downward. If you experience depression, the Bible promises that God will see, hear, and save you.

Elijah, a biblical prophet, let emotional fear throw his life out of balance. Queen Jezebel threatened to kill Elijah when he opposed her idol worship. Elijah was consumed with fear and fled for his life into the wilderness. "It is enough; now, O LORD, take away my life" (1 Kings 19:4, NRSV). God sent the angel of the Lord to care for his physical needs, then He dealt with Elijah's emotional and spiritual needs. God was faithful to lift Elijah from his depression, and He will be faithful to you, too.

David, a shepherd who grew up to be a king, also knew what depression was like. Many times he turned to God, pouring out his feelings in prayer. Even when David approached God with sadness, God uplifted David's spirit and gave him hope. God's promise to answer and rescue David from despair is evident throughout the Psalms. He did it for David, and He will do it for you.

worth thinking about

► **Need your** life-light recharged? God can do it. "You light a lamp for me. The LORD, my God, lights up my darkness" (Psalm 18:28, NLT).

► **A dose of** psalms is good medicine. Discover God's promises. "You, O LORD, are a shield around me, my glory, and the one who lifts up my head" (Psalm 3:3, NRSV).

► **Learn a new song.** "He lifted me out of the slimy pit, out of the mud and mire; he set my feet on a rock and gave me a firm place to stand. He put a new song in my mouth" (Psalm 40:2–3, NIV).

Why are you downcast, O my soul? Why so disturbed within me? Put your hope in God, for I will yet praise him, my Savior and my God.

Psalm 42:11, NIV

30

Will God's promises help you with tough situations?

When the terrain of life is rough, how can the bumpy places be made smooth? A person cannot go back and live life over. How can life's difficulties be resolved when a person is responsible for many of the mistakes? Where can the solution to life's dilemmas be found? Will God help someone who has not been walking closely to Him? Will He provide the answers to life's impossible circumstances? Will His promises help you in your tough situations?

answer

Part of being human is finding yourself in troubling circumstances—some of your own making and some not. But God says, "Call upon me in the day of trouble; I will deliver you, and you will honor me" (Psalm 50:15, NIV). Not only is that a great promise, but there is more. God is able to bring good out of negative situations. "We know that all things work together for good for those who love God, who are called according to his purpose" (Romans 8:28, NRSV). Simply put, when you turn and search for Him with your heart, you will find Him. He will be there to help you make sense of your life. This does not mean He will remove the consequences of poor choices or make your life problem-free. But it does mean that He will be there to help you. Often He uses adversity and affliction to shape you into the person He knows you can become.

Although you cannot go back and live life over, God gives some wise advice regarding the past: "Forget about what's happened; don't keep going over old history. Be alert, be present. I'm about to do something brand-new. It's bursting out! Don't you see it? There it is! I'm making a road through the desert, rivers in the badlands" (Isaiah 43:18–19, THE MESSAGE). God does not want you to live in regret. He wants you to look to Him and follow His lead.

worth thinking about

- ▶ **Try getting** the focus off yourself. Ask God to put someone in your path whom you can help. Recognizing and supplying another's need often lifts your spirit.

- ▶ **Do talk to God.** Take a prayer walk and pour out your heart in conversation to God. Ask Him to supply your needs.

- ▶ **Practice giving** your problems to God. Type them on your computer, and then delete all of them. If you start worrying again, repeat the process. Soon you will be able to stop worrying and leave your problems with God.

> *Do not be afraid—I am with you! I am your God—let nothing terrify you! I will make you strong and help you; I will protect you and save you.*
> Isaiah 41:10, GNT

question

Does God promise to help you make wise decisions?

Decision making is tough for most people. But a small segment of the population seems to be able to decide with confidence. What is the secret in deciding so swiftly and assuredly? It is almost like decisive people have a magic formula. Personally, you do not have the first clue as to how to make a wise decision. Does the Bible give any guidance for making wise decisions? If so, what is it? Does God promise to help?

answer

James, a biblical writer, said, "If you don't know what you're doing, pray to the Father. He loves to help. You'll get his help, and won't be condescended to when you ask for it" (James 1:5, THE MESSAGE). Asking God for guidance should be the beginning point in all decision making.

God will never lead you to make a decision that is unkind, immoral, or illegal. Three key questions will guide you in decision making: Does your choice line up with God's teachings? Do circumstances indicate that you are moving in the right direction? And do you have an inner peace about your decision?

God wanted Jonah to go to Nineveh and warn the people to change their ways. Jonah made a wrong decision. Not only did he bring on a storm in his life, but those in the boat with him chose to throw him overboard to save their lives. A giant fish swallowed him. God kept him safe in the belly of the whale until he reconsidered his decision.

If the answers to the three key questions are negative, then look for another choice. Make wise decisions and have peace. Choose poorly and endure painful consequences.

worth thinking about

▶ **The Israelites** let fear keep them from making the right decision. They were afraid to claim the Promised Land. Instead, they wandered in the wilderness for forty years and missed God's blessing.

▶ **A woman** named Rahab made the right decision to be kind to God's people and hide them from the spies. She and her family were saved from harm.

▶ **Joseph refused** the advances of Pharaoh's wife because he knew it would go against the moral laws of God. Pharaoh believed his wife and imprisoned Joseph. God used this as a detour on Joseph's way to success.

> *Don't become so well-adjusted to your culture that you fit into it without even thinking. Instead, fix your attention on God. You'll be changed from the inside out. Readily recognize what he wants from you, and quickly respond to it.*
>
> Romans 12:2, THE MESSAGE

32

question

Do God's promises help you make the right decision?

Struggling over a decision can be difficult. A person's head often leads one way while his heart leads another. Discussing choices with friends can prove futile, for they may be split in their opinions. Listing the pros and cons regarding a difficult decision does not always work either, because human nature tends to overrule the least favorite choice. Where can a person find help for this taxing problem? Will God's promises help a person make the right choice?

answer

Decision making is difficult because people look at what will make them happy in the moment instead of considering the long-term effect. People want what they want right now! Paul, a worker for God and the writer of many books in the Bible, said that there is a constant war between the human spirit and the flesh. People often know the right decision, but they may choose exactly the opposite.

God is the first to consult when making a decision. Ask God for His guidance and strength to make the right choice. It is all right to get the opinions of others, but consider whom you ask. Have they made wise choices in their lives? Unwise counselors have destroyed many kings and nations.

God gives a promise you can count on in Proverbs 3. If you trust in God with all your heart and do not try to decide without Him, He will help you by pointing you in the right way. Do not try to be wise in your own eyes, for another proverb reads, "There is a path before each person that seems right, but it ends in death" (Proverbs 14:12, NLT). God promises to help you when you trust Him and enlist His help in making decisions.

worth thinking about

- ▶ **Begin with God.** King Solomon told God that he did not know the first thing about being a ruler. He asked for discernment and the wisdom to rule the people justly.

- ▶ **Choose experienced** counselors. Solomon's son, King Rehoboam, let himself be influenced by his peers rather than listen to his father's experienced counselors. The people rebelled.

- ▶ **Ask God** to strengthen your spirit. Samson was a strong man who lived in Old Testament days. His attraction to Delilah, who worked for his enemy, the Philistines, was his downfall. Samson chose flesh over his inner nudging.

I pray that your love will keep on growing more and more, together with true knowledge and perfect judgment, so that you will be able to choose what is best.

Philippians 1:9–10, GNT

33

question

Does God promise to guide you?

Everyone says just ask God to help you make decisions. They make it sound so easy. But how can you be sure He will help? Does He promise to guide you? What if you think you've heard God but it was really your own inclination? What if you do not understand His direction? Does it just come down to an issue of trust? The whole process of decision making leaves you bewildered. What does the Bible teach regarding the promise of guidance?

answer

"By your words I can see where I'm going; they throw a beam of light on my dark path" (Psalm 119:105, THE MESSAGE). Reading the Bible and knowing what God teaches will shine light upon your decision-making process—just as a flashlight shines light on your path. It is hard to make decisions without knowing what God desires for you. All God's principles are based on wisdom and given for your good. "You're blessed when you stay on course, walking steadily on the road revealed by GOD" (Psalm 119:1, THE MESSAGE).

Faith (trust) is a factor in whether you stick with a decision that you have made. The people of Israel believed

God would hold back the Red Sea until they passed through. If they had not believed, they might have turned back and been destroyed. God promises to guide you, and He will. But if you start questioning His guidance, you may also question your decision.

Over and over the Bible teaches that God will guide you when you ask. Scripture also reveals that God always keeps His promises. He is still keeping them today. He promises to be your teacher and guide you with His counsel.

worth thinking about

▶ **Do your homework.** "All Scripture is inspired by God and is useful to teach us what is true and to make us realize what is wrong in our lives. It corrects us when we are wrong and teaches us to do what is right" (2 Timothy 3:16, NLT).

▶ **Seek God's counsel.** "Don't worry about anything, but in all your prayers ask God for what you need, always asking him with a thankful heart" (Philippians 4:6, GNT).

▶ **Decide to trust.** Sometimes it is that simple. The choice is yours, just as it was in biblical times. You choose whether you believe God's promise for guidance.

> *Trust in the LORD with all your heart, and do not rely on your own insight. In all your ways acknowledge him, and he will make straight your paths.*
> Proverbs 3:5–6, NRSV

question
▼
Will God's promised guidance allow you choices?

People struggle over job decisions that require them to relocate, wondering if it is the right choice. Does God care where people live geographically? Does He care about the houses they live in or the cars they drive? Does He even care about their career or marriage choices? One person says that God has a plan for each life; another insists that God gave mankind the freedom to decide things for themselves. How can both be right? Which is true?

answer
▼

Jeremiah, a prophet of God, said that God does have a plan for your life. "Surely I know the plans I have for you, says the LORD, plans for your welfare and not for harm, to give you a future with hope" (Jeremiah 29:11, NRSV). When you were just a thought in His mind, before you were ever formed in your mother's womb, God decided what personality you would have. God planned what talents and special abilities He would give to you. "Your eyes saw my unformed body. All the days ordained for me were written in your book before one of them came to be" (Psalm 139:16, NIV).

God does have specific plans for you regarding major matters such as marriage, lifework, and your geographical location. The decisions He guides you to are His specific choices for definite time periods in your life. They fit with His perfect plan and promises for you.

At the same time, God wants you to be free to choose whether you will let Him be God of your life. He will not force Himself on anyone. God does not care if you drive a red or blue car. Of course, He is delighted when you seek His guidance on such matters. He always wants to guide you to good things; He wants you to be happy. God does have a plan for your life, and He does give you choices—both of these statements are true.

worth thinking about

▶ **God chose** a wife for Israel's leader, Isaac. A servant was sent to their homeland. The servant prayed, and God guided him to the right girl. Everyone involved had choices to make.

▶ **God had a plan** for Solomon's life. He was to be king and was to build God's temple. Solomon had choices along the way.

▶ **God had a plan** for Paul's ministry. "During the night, Paul had a vision of someone from Macedonia who was standing there and begging him, 'Come over to Macedonia and help us!'" (Acts 16:9, CEV). Paul had a choice on whether he obeyed.

> *The God of our ancestors has chosen you to know his will, to see the Righteous One and to hear his own voice.*
>
> Acts 22:14, NRSV

question

Will God's promises help you overcome your fear of decision making?

People often procrastinate when important decisions have to be made because they do not know what to do. The fear of making a wrong decision paralyzes them. They try to put off resolving the situation as long as possible, but eventually their hands will be forced. They'll have to decide what they're going to do. Can God help them overcome their fears and quit worrying about making wrong decisions? What promises will enable them to trust and not be afraid?

answer

The only kind of wrong decision that you can make is one that goes against God's laws and principles. The Bible is your guide for making decisions that matter. It is there that you learn about God's laws and principles for living. God promises that He will guide you when you ask, and He will. You do not have to be afraid of making the wrong decision when you decide with God.

Remind yourself that choices about which outfit to wear, what furniture to buy, or what style of house to live in are not wrong unless you're disregarding one of God's principles about money. Those choices deal with your personal preferences.

Stop and ask yourself, what is the worst thing that can happen if you unintentionally make a decision that goes against God's principles? You simply tell Him, ask Him to forgive you, and ask Him to help get you back on track. There may be consequences that result from a wrong choice, but God will be there with you and help you find your way. Peter, a disciple of Jesus, made a wrong decision when he denied Jesus. Peter acted out of fear and on his own. But even then Jesus didn't leave him in a state of regret. Jesus and Peter talked. Jesus forgave Peter and assigned an important job for him to do. You cannot go wrong when you decide with God.

worth thinking about

▶ **Let trust chase** fear away. Repeat God's promises to love you, guide you, and never leave you, until His promises become a part of you.

▶ **Consider who God** is, the one true God who is all-knowing. He knows exactly what you should do. You only have to ask, and He will tell you.

▶ **Fear does not** come from God. If you're experiencing fear regarding a decision, ask God to help you decide in faith: Is your decision against His principles? Do circumstances agree with your choice? Do you have peace about your decision? Follow His leading.

Why are you so afraid?
Do you still have no faith?
Mark 4:40, NIV

question

How can anyone find the truth?

answer

When the Friend comes, the Spirit of the Truth, he will take you by the hand and guide you into all the truth there is.

John 16:13, THE MESSAGE

36

Do God's promises encourage you to seek advice?

The decision-making process for many people involves asking everyone around them what they should do. Those who are trying to decide hope the tally of votes will guide them. But this method does not work; rather, it eliminates the votes of the people whose opinions they do not value, and tosses out those who might not have understood. The opinion-seekers wish that God spoke audibly. They continually question if it is okay to seek other people's opinions regarding decisions. What does God say about this matter?

answer

God spoke aloud to Samuel in Old Testament times, so anything is possible. But it is true that today God's Spirit generally speaks in your mind, through the Bible, or by way of circumstances. God desires that you seek His advice first and foremost. Again and again He tells you to call on Him through prayer.

But it is okay to ask other people's opinions because God does desire that His followers share what they have learned with one another. Scripture promises that God is with you, but He often sends someone who has gone through an experience similar to yours. "He comes alongside us when we go through hard times, and before you know it, he brings us alongside someone else who is going through hard times so that we can be there for that person just as God was there for us" (2 Corinthians 1:4, THE MESSAGE). The promises found in the Book of Proverbs encourage you to search out those who can give good advice. Proverbs 18:4 says that a person's words can be a source of wisdom.

When you ask someone for guidance in making a particular decision, you must be sure that he is qualified to give you an answer. Wise decisions are based on God's principles. It is smart to ask God to place someone in your path who can help you think through your decision.

worth thinking about

- ▶ **God is almighty**, but He is also a friend. God talked and listened to Abraham as God and as a friend regarding the destruction of Sodom and Gomorrah.

- ▶ **Ask God to** give you a wise and trusted friend. David and Jonathan were two friends who lived in biblical times. Both of them loved God. Their friendship enabled them to get through difficult decisions together.

- ▶ **Search out** those who know the Scriptures when seeking advice. "The mouths of the righteous utter wisdom. . . . The law of their God is in their hearts; their steps do not slip" (Psalm 37:30–31, NRSV).

> *Arrogant know-it-alls stir up discord, but wise men and women listen to each other's counsel.*
> Proverbs 13:10, THE MESSAGE

question

▼

Why doesn't God promise to tell you exactly what to do?

Most people agree that when they are trying to make a decision, it would be simpler if God would call them on the phone and talk to them personally. Then they could clearly hear His voice regarding the decision they have to make. If He would send an e-mail or a letter, it would be so much easier. Sometimes people get so enmeshed in the decision-making process that they miss what God is trying to tell them. Why doesn't God just tell people what to do?

answer

▼

There are several reasons God does not tell you what to do. Here are three reasons: First, He has given you free will. You are not a puppet, and you do have choices. Second, God wants you to go to Him and seek His guidance through prayer and Bible reading. God has principles and laws to help you in your decision making, but He will never force you. Third, He wants you to calm down and listen, and He wants you to learn to discern His leading. He is constantly leading and teaching you the right way to go.

The prophet Elijah was overwhelmed with fear concerning his problems. He ran away and hid in a cave. God told him to go out and stand on the mountain, for God was going to pass by. A mighty wind roared by, but God was not in the wind. Then there was an earthquake, but God was not in the earthquake. Next there was a fire, but God was not in the fire. "And after the fire came a gentle whisper. When Elijah heard it, he pulled his cloak over his face and went out and stood at the mouth of the cave" (1 Kings 19:12–13, NIV). God was in the gentle whisper. That is why it is imperative that you calm your spirit and relax. Often, you will hear God speak your guidance in a gentle whisper.

worth thinking about

▶ **Take a break.** Do something for fun and relaxation, but keep a spiritual ear tuned to God. You'll hear the gentle whisper when you are least expecting it, and you will know what to do.

▶ **Look around** you. What are the signposts in your circumstances? Sometimes, God is all but sending an e-mail or a letter straight from heaven.

▶ **Listen to other** people. Sometimes God speaks through them. You do not even have to ask them about your decision. God will surprise you by making their words apply to your situation.

> *When the Spirit of truth comes, he will guide you into all truth. He will not speak on his own but will tell you what he has heard. He will tell you about the future.*
> John 16:13, NLT

question

Does God promise to help you discern right and wrong?

One person may think that a certain decision is okay, while another person suggests that the same decision is morally wrong. Someone else calls it a gray area and believes each person has to decide what's right for himself. People often find themselves questioning a decision as they wrestle with their conscience and try to decide if it is ethical. Does God help people discern what is morally right and what is morally wrong? Will God's promises guide you to make the honorable choice?

answer

All God's laws and principles were given to help you live the good life and not bear the consequences of wrong decisions. Knowing God's promises will give you discernment, which is recognizing what is right in God's sight and what pleases Him, as well as knowing what displeases Him. Your ability to discern right from wrong will become sharper as you study the Bible. Prayer plays a part in discernment, too, because when you ask, God will answer.

God promises to teach you and help you recognize right from wrong according to His laws. He promises that if you start to go the wrong way, He will guide you back to the right way. Scripture points out that He will never lead you to do anything dishonest because it is not His nature. He will never lead you to harm another person because God created you in His image. He will never tempt you to do wrong.

Another way that God teaches discernment is through the biblical stories given in the Bible. These stories tell of the decisions made by people who lived long ago. They reveal how God interacted with them. The same principles God used to guide them are still applicable to your life today.

worth thinking about

▶ **Knowing the laws** of the road and obeying them will help you travel safely. Knowing God's laws and obeying them will give you joy and spare you unpleasant consequences.

▶ **Assembling a bicycle** without reading the directions will leave you with leftover parts, and the bicycle may never work as the manufacturer intended. Making life decisions without reading the Scriptures will cause you to miss good things in your life.

▶ **Ignoring the car** manual's recommendation for oil changes will burn up the motor. Ignoring the need to fill up spiritually with wisdom from God's Bible will cause the light of your life to burn low.

Direct my footsteps according to your word; let no sin rule over me. Redeem me from the oppression of men, that I may obey your precepts.
Psalm 119:133–134, NIV

39

question

▼

How does God reveal His promised guidance?

God remains silent, even after you have prayed and prayed. Doesn't He know that you have a decision to make and that you need His input? You're feeling frantic and desperate. The decision has to be made soon. Why is God leaving you in limbo when you're trying to do what's right by seeking His guidance? Why is He ignoring your request? Does He not care? What is His purpose in making you wait? Why is God delaying His direction?

answer

▼

God is in control, even when you cannot feel His hand of direction. He is always guiding; you have His promise. "The LORD will guide you continually, and satisfy your needs in parched places" (Isaiah 58:11, NRSV). If He is withholding a definite directive, it may be because the timing is not right. You may be sitting at a stoplight in life where God says, "Wait!"

Perhaps God's purpose in delaying the specific guidance you are seeking is to grow your trust in Him. It is important to remember that God is never late. He is always on time with His guidance. Choosing to trust that God is leading will enable you to release your anxiety. "Don't be afraid, for I am with you. Don't be discouraged, for I am your God. I will strengthen you and help you. I will hold you up with my victorious right hand" (Isaiah 41:10, NLT). Trust that God is guiding, and you may realize that His answer is right in front of you. Anxiety has a way of putting blinders on your eyes and earplugs in your ears. You may not have recognized God's leading.

If God is directing you to wait, do not rush ahead. The secret to the waiting is in the believing. If you take God at His word—that He is guiding even though you cannot see or feel His leading—you can wait with expectation.

worth thinking about

▶ **Stop and wait** for God. Abraham and Sarah grew impatient. God had promised Abraham many descendants. They decided to help God out, and Abraham fathered a child by Sarah's maid. This wasn't the promised heir, and many problems arose from their rushing ahead.

▶ **Yield to God's** commands and wait faithfully. The Israelites didn't wait for Moses to return. They gave in to their feelings of abandonment, and many died.

▶ **Do not pass** up God's laws. Impatient Saul didn't wait for God's prophet Samuel before offering a sacrifice. His disobedience cost him his kingdom.

> *Wait patiently for the LORD. Be brave and courageous. Yes, wait patiently for the LORD.*
> Psalm 27:14, NLT

question

▼

Does God promise peace if you've made the right decision?

The decision is made. There is no turning back. You were excited about your decision until *wham!* One circumstance after another hit you in the face, making you wonder if you'd heard God wrong. Although all indicators had been a go and you'd made your decision with confidence, now you're puzzled. Were you listening to your own selfish wants and only thought you heard God's voice? Is God testing you to see if you trust Him? Will God help you cope with your fears and doubts?

answer

▼

Matthew, a disciple of Jesus, wrote one of the books of the Bible. He told how Jesus sent His disciples to get in a boat and cross a lake. Jesus went up on the hillside to pray. Toward morning, strong winds rocked the boat. Jesus saw the problem and started toward the disciples, walking on the water.

The men were frightened and thought the shape they saw might be a ghost. Jesus called out, telling them not to be afraid. Peter, a disciple, asked Jesus to call to him. Jesus did, and Peter started walking on the water. A sudden gust of wind caused Peter to take his eyes off Jesus, and he began to sink. "Immediately Jesus reached out his hand and caught him. 'You of little faith,' he said, 'why did you doubt?'" (Matthew 14:31, NIV).

There are several things to be learned from this story. Jesus told the disciples to get in the boat. It was the right decision. Jesus was watching all along. When trouble came, it was Jesus who rescued them. Peter could do the impossible when his focus was on Jesus. But when he took his eyes off Jesus, he sank. Immediately Jesus grabbed him and kept him from going under.

Sometimes, after making the right decision, trouble may arrive in some form. It is imperative to remember not to take your eyes off Jesus, but if you do have doubt or fear, He will rescue you as He did Peter.

worth thinking about

▶ **Step out** in trust. "Without faith it is impossible to please God" (Hebrews 11:6, NRSV). Jesus told mankind that they would have trouble in this world, but He is in control.

▶ **Walk on** in faith. "We walk by faith, not by sight" (2 Corinthians 5:7, NRSV). God wants you to believe that He will enable you to do what He has called you to do.

▶ **Keep your focus** on Jesus and not on the threatening trouble. If you view only your problems, they will look larger and larger.

> *I am confident of this, that the one who began a good work among you will bring it to completion by the day of Jesus Christ.*
> Philippians 1:6, NRSV

41

question

How can God's promises strengthen your family?

Some of your kids' friends are involved in church activities, and they have invited your children to join them. Although your family hasn't attended church, you suppose it is okay. Truthfully, you'd rather not have to get up on your day off. Still, it feels like the right thing to do. So you and your husband are going to make an effort to get a Sunday morning church routine started. Will attending church help your family learn God's promises? Will His promises strengthen your family?

answer

God promises that He will give good things to those who follow His commands. "If you listen to these commands and obey them faithfully, then the LORD your God will continue to keep his covenant with you and will show you his constant love" (Deuteronomy 7:12, GNT). God's laws help a family keep their priorities straight. There is no misunderstanding about what is important or acceptable. The reality is that a family is a unit, and the choices of one member will affect everyone else in the group. Mistakes are forgiven, but families that seek to please God are more apt to avoid painful mistakes.

Families who are working to live up to God's principles are blessed by God and strengthened by their united commitment.

One of God's laws is to remember the Sabbath. Paul, a New Testament writer, said that God's people need to meet together so they can bolster one another. This holds true for individual families as well as for the entire family of believers. Joining with other believers will strengthen your family, and each member will receive guidance for daily living.

When families learn how God protected those who lived in biblical times, they will recognize God's power and grow in faith.

worth thinking about

▶ **Knowing God's laws** and the promises that will come from obedience will fortify your family members with courage. They are more likely to make the best decision when they have God's guidance.

▶ **A thankful family** might choose to serve together in some form of community service. Obeying God's command to love others will strengthen and bless the family unit.

▶ **When families know** that God promised never to leave them and that He will always protect His people, they will be able to face crises in His strength.

> My health may fail, and my spirit may grow weak, but God remains the strength of my heart; he is mine forever.
>
> Psalm 73:26, NLT

42

question

What promise does God give if you honor your parents?

One of the Ten Commandments is to honor your father and mother. Exactly what does that involve? Does it mean that you need to be obedient from birth to eternity? More likely it means to always treat them with respect. Naturally, that's your desire, for your parents are responsible for your birth. God must deem it a high priority if He made it one of the top ten laws. Does He give any promises in regard to honoring your parents?

answer

This commandment, number five, ranks in the first half of God's top-ten laws. "Respect your father and your mother, and you will live a long time in the land I am giving you" (Exodus 20:12, CEV). Your relationship with your earthly parents—how you esteem them—is a foundation builder and reflection of your relationship with God. If you do not learn to obey an earthly authority, you will never be able to obey a heavenly one. If you do not learn from your parents how to stick to a task, you will never be able to apply yourself to God's work. Honoring your parents is for your good. By doing so you will become the person God intends you to be.

The second part of the commandment does promise a long life. The laws were originally given to the Israelites as they journeyed to the Promised Land. But they are promises for all time, for all who love the Lord. Treating your parents with respect makes God smile on you. Paul, a worker for God, wrote the following in a letter to the Ephesians: "'Honor your father and mother'—this is the first commandment with a promise: 'so that it may be well with you and you may live long on the earth'" (Ephesians 6:2–3, NRSV).

worth thinking about

► Visiting with your parents and listening to them as they share their past memories is one way to show respect. You may be amazed at what you will learn. God promises to lengthen your days and bless you.

► Being patient with your parents when their walk has slowed and their hearing has failed is showing respect. God promises that when you honor them, things will go well for you.

► Respecting your parents' opinions even if you do not agree will please God and bring His promised blessings.

> Listen to your father who begot you, and do not despise your mother when she is old.
> Proverbs 23:22, NRSV

43

What promises does God give to parents?

Parenting is one of the toughest jobs in the world. The entire extended family is generally involved in the rearing of a child. Everyone desires to do a good job, but it is serious business. Some claim that if you give it your best that is all that's required. But what if your best falls short? You want to know for sure that you are doing the right thing. What does the Bible teach regarding child rearing? Does God have any promises for training children?

answer

God loves children. He has given parents, along with the extended family, the responsibility of teaching children about His laws. "Bring them up in the discipline and instruction of the Lord" (Ephesians 6:4, NRSV). Knowing the principles and living by them will enable parents and everyone involved in child rearing to raise their children confidently. The promise is given in Psalm 102 that the children of God's people will live in security, even unto the next generation.

God helps parents by giving them sound advice with this promise: "Teach children how they should live, and they will remember it all their life" (Proverbs 22:6, GNT). This does not mean that there will never be a period in your children's lives where they won't defy your teaching. But it does suggest that if they rebel for a time, the foundational training they received will come to mind and correct their rebellious nature.

God adds another important piece of advice for parents. "Fathers, do not aggravate your children, or they will become discouraged" (Colossians 3:21, NLT). Children are instructed to be obedient and respectful, but parents also have a responsibility. Nagging produces rebellion. Discipline is used to bring about a desired behavior. Punishment is generally cruel and has to do with making someone pay for a mistake. Courtesy and patient teaching will produce cooperative children.

worth thinking about

▶ **Children learn** by observing. When you live by God's principles and laws, your children are more likely to do the same.

▶ **Children cannot** obey what they aren't taught. Psalm 78 says to tell your children about how God has worked in the past and is still working in your life, and your family will be blessed.

▶ **Parents who take** the time to follow God's directives will bring blessings to themselves and to others. Children who are taught proper manners and behavior are pleasant to be around, and they bring peace to the family as well as joy to others.

> *All your children shall be taught by the LORD, and great shall be the prosperity of your children.*
> Isaiah 54:13, NRSV

question

Will God's promises help your family work out their differences?

Every family is a mix of personalities and temperaments, but some blend together better than others. If the temperaments clash, there can be major discord. A home is supposed to be a haven for each family member. But where there is constant bickering or arguing, there can be no peace. Can God help your family resolve their differences and get along with one another? Does God give any promises that will help your family live in peace?

answer

God values peace. Jesus promised this: "You're blessed when you can show people how to cooperate instead of compete or fight. That's when you discover who you really are, and your place in God's family" (Matthew 5:9, THE MESSAGE). Paul, God's missionary, tells you to pursue peace (Romans 14:19).

When a family invites God into their home, God is free to begin to work through each family member to establish His peace. True peace cannot exist apart from God. When God is at the center of a family, members desire to please Him by living according to His principles and laws.

Paul wrote, "Get rid of all bitterness, passion, and anger. No more shouting or insults, no more hateful feelings of any sort. Instead, be kind and tender-hearted to one another, and forgive one another, as God has forgiven you through Christ" (Ephesians 4:31–32, GNT). A good place to put God's commandments into practice is in the home. As family members grow in their walk with God, they will choose to get rid of the ugly feelings faster and be quicker to forgive. Your home will become more and more peaceful. Family members will strive to overlook one another's faults and live together peacefully in spite of different personalities.

worth thinking about

▶ **Avoid self-centeredness** like the plague. The Bible says that jealousy and selfishness cause disorder and evil. Scripture promises that living by God's laws will produce a harvest of good (James 3:13–18).

▶ **Love others**, and you will live in the light of God's goodness. If you allow bitter or hateful feelings to enter your life, darkness will surround you (1 John 2:9–11).

▶ **Encourage family** members to speak positive words to one another. "Words kill, words give life; they're either poison or fruit—you choose" (Proverbs 18:21, THE MESSAGE).

> *How wonderful, how beautiful, when brothers and sisters get along!...It's like the dew on Mount Hermon flowing down the slopes of Zion. Yes, that's where GOD commands the blessing, ordains eternal life.*
>
> Psalm 133:1, 3, THE MESSAGE

question

How do God's promises teach families to respect others?

People question if respect is still being taught in schools. But the foundation for respect is laid even before children enter school. It begins in the home. Society does not make teaching respect easy, and parents have a difficult task. TV shows and movies often set poor examples. Although it is a parent's choice as to what is permitted, it is difficult and unwise to totally insulate the family from the world. Will God's promises help teach the family to respect others?

answer

Respect is treating others with consideration and esteem. The practice of respect begins in the home. If it is not taught there, family members won't know how to show respect to God, to other people, or to those who are in positions of authority. Respect does not mean that you always agree with people, but it means that you honor them as children of God. That may mean respectfully closing your mouth and submitting to their authority.

God promises that you will live long and that things will go well for you when you respect others (Deuteronomy 5 and 6). When a family turns to God for help in teaching respect, then His commandments will clearly instruct them as to His expectations. When family members understand why they are to be respectful—because God commands it—and what the promised blessings are, they will be more likely to comply.

What are God's rules of respect? The Scriptures say, "Respect everyone, and love your Christian brothers and sisters. Fear God, and respect the king" (1 Peter 2:17, NLT). That just about covers it. In addition, you are to show respect for older people and honor them, and show respect for foreigners who are living in your land. It is plain to see, God intends for you to treat everyone with consideration. Families who make it a habit to show respect in the home will honor God and draw His promised blessings.

worth thinking about

▶ Respect means not demanding your own way. It means considering another's needs above your own. When you show respect, you will reap a blessing from God's promise that things will go well for you.

▶ Respect means to show honor to those who have lived longer and experienced more of life. When you openly listen to their opinions, you are honoring them. God promises to bless you with a long life.

▶ Respect means honoring those in authority. You submit to their decisions out of respect for their positions.

Remember these commands and cherish them. . . . Then you and your children will live a long time in the land that the LORD your God promised to your ancestors. You will live there as long as there is a sky above the earth.
Deuteronomy 11:18, 21, GNT

question

What if a person follows all God's laws?

answer

If you pay attention to these laws and are careful to follow them, then the LORD your God . . . will love you and bless you and increase your numbers.

Deuteronomy 7:12–13, NIV

46

question

▼

How do God's promises produce supportive families?

The world can be a tough place. People in the world are not always supportive of one another. Still, all people need a place where they are accepted for who they are. They need a place where they can receive encouragement when they're having trouble and applause when they've done their best. The home needs to be that place. How can family members show support for one another? Will following God's commands and knowing His promises produce supportive families?

answer

▼

When a family chooses to follow God's commandments, He will fill them with His compassion and kindness for others. They will want to start in the home to be encouraging. The promise for being supportive to your family and to others is one given throughout the Scriptures. God will bless your life with good things when you obey His laws and principles for living.

There will be numerous occasions, and different ways, that family members can show their support for one another, including by their choice of words. "Kind words are like honey—they cheer you up and make you feel strong" (Proverbs 16:24, CEV). Supportive words are bound to spur a family member on to success. God says to speak positive words, not worthless words. He desires that you use words that build up self-esteem and not use words that tear down a person's self-worth.

Another way family members can support one another is by being there. When you choose to attend an activity or the special event of a family member, you are giving the gift of support. But there are those times that come to everyone when words are insufficient. A family member may have suffered a deep hurt. It is in those situations that your quiet presence at a family member's side speaks volumes. Following God's commandments will produce supportive families.

worth thinking about

- ▶ Support a family member's dream. God has a plan for each life. He nudges people to that plan by placing dreams within them. God will bless you when you cheer them on.

- ▶ Encourage a family member by assisting with a difficult task. God has given everyone different skills. When you support another by giving of your abilities, God will reward you.

- ▶ Lend a sympathetic ear and listen to a family member's problem. The Bible says that God gives people to each other so they can be mutually encouraged.

> Let us be concerned for one another, to help one another to show love and to do good.
> Hebrews 10:24, GNT

question

What promises help family members forgive one another?

Family is a joy whenever everyone is getting along, but when they're not, look out! How can people that have been placed in the same family unit begin life by loving one another and then refuse to forgive each other? Nothing can be gained when a family is split, for the entire family unit is affected by the actions of one or two members. Does God give promises in the Bible that will enable family members to forgive each other?

answer

God created families and placed you in yours for a lifetime. You may branch off and start another family unit, but you will always be a part of the family you were born into. It is in your original family unit that you first began to learn how to live in peace with others. Family living prepares you for interaction in the world as you reach adulthood.

Too frequently, major clashes occur in the lifetime of a family. Arguments may break out, and family members may reach an impasse. If hurt feelings are nursed, family members may find it impossible to forgive one another. Everyone in the family will lose, for all family gatherings will be tainted by this attitude. Eventually the relationship of the entire family unit will be destroyed. This is the time that a family needs to look to God's promises to find out how He wants them to handle the situation.

Jesus told His disciples to forgive seventy times seven, meaning that they should never stop. "Put up with each other, and forgive anyone who does you wrong, just as Christ has forgiven you. Love is more important than anything else. It is what ties everything completely together" (Colossians 3:13–14, CEV). Jesus has set the example of forgiveness, which families are to follow. God has promised forgiveness to mankind when they choose Him, and He likewise commands them to forgive others.

worth thinking about

- ▶ **Do not take** sides. "Don't argue just to be arguing, when you haven't been hurt" (Proverbs 3:30, CEV).

- ▶ **Love as God** loves. Forgive wrongs and encourage other family members to do the same. Let God be your model.

- ▶ **Keep the answers** to your prayers flowing. "When you stand praying, if you hold anything against anyone, forgive him, so that your Father in heaven may forgive you your sins" (Mark 11:25, NIV).

> *Be merciful, just as your Father is merciful. Do not judge, and you will not be judged; do not condemn, and you will not be condemned. Forgive, and you will be forgiven.*
>
> Luke 6:36–37, NRSV

48

question

Does God have promises for the blended family?

The only certainty in life is change. This is not only evident in nature, but in relationships as well. Death and divorce often take their toll on families, and the structures of families change. When partners with children choose to remarry, the blended family is born. Many adjustments have to be made, and the effect is felt throughout the entire extended family. Does God have any promises that will make living in a blended family easier? If so, what are they?

answer

God does have promises for those who are beginning anew. One involves looking to the future and being excited about it! "The LORD says, 'Do not cling to events of the past or dwell on what happened long ago. Watch for the new thing I am going to do'" (Isaiah 43:18–19, GNT). This does not mean that you are to forget your first family, but it does mean that you are to focus on the future.

Realize that God will help you grow through the changes in your family and become the person He created you to be. There will be troubling times as well as joyful times in your new family, but it won't be because of being in a blended family. Life is just that way. The situations might have been different, but there would have still been high and low places in the lives of your original family unit.

God is able to do anything. He has the ability to take two factions and unite them into one. He did it in the Bible, and He will do it for your blended family. "He himself is our peace, who has made the two one and has destroyed the barrier, the dividing wall of hostility" (Ephesians 2:14, NIV). God will smooth out the difficult situations and bless your blended household as one fam-ily. When you follow His leading, He will bless your family. That's His promise to you.

worth thinking about

▶ Stretch your patience and try to get along with new family members. God has called you to live in peace, and to make allowances for each person's faults (Ephesians 4:2–3). The result will be a happy blended family.

▶ Accept your chance for a new beginning. God has brought you into a new time, a new place, and has a plan for this period of your life.

▶ Live expecting good things to come your way. When you choose God's way, He promises to send good things your way.

> *Above all, love each other deeply, because love covers over a multitude of sins.*
> 1 Peter 4:8, NIV

question

What promises keep a family on God's path?

Raising a family in today's culture is not an easy task. The family can be going down the right road completely unaware that unacceptable behaviors and habits are taking root. How can you keep more in tune with the family's direction when you're busy making a living? Sometimes it is too easy to follow the mainstream of society without questioning where they're going, but your family deserves better. Does God have promises that will keep you from mindlessly following the crowd?

answer

"Do not be conformed to this world, but be transformed by the renewing of your minds, so that you may discern what is the will of God—what is good and acceptable and perfect" (Romans 12:2, NRSV). God's people are not to walk blindly, following the standards of this world, but to walk according to God's laws and principles.

Unfortunately, the evil in this world constantly tries to slip something into society under the guise of its being good. If you do not know God's promises and commandments, you will fall for these ploys and take your family down with you. There will be consequences to pay.

Paul warned God's followers: "I insist—and God backs me up on this—that there be no going along with the crowd, the empty-headed, mindless crowd. They've refused for so long to deal with God that they've lost touch not only with God but with reality itself. They can't think straight anymore" (Ephesians 4:17–19, THE MESSAGE). If you want to keep your family on God's path, you must choose to be alert to what's happening in society. Mindless living will only bring you pain. Ask God to help you discern what is right for your family. God promises to keep you on His path when you choose to follow His commandments.

worth thinking about

▶ **Do your homework.** "The LORD gives wisdom" (Proverbs 2:6, NIV). Learn what the Lord expects; discover His promises and commandments for a good life.

▶ **Identify with** family groups that focus on God's purposes. Their aim is to stay current on what is happening in the world. But be sure to let God's Spirit be your final guide. Even God's followers can be led astray.

▶ **Be consistent** in following God's ways. Do not say something is not right, and then give in when you're tired or under pressure. Ask God to help you stand firm on His principles.

> *Dear friend, take my advice; it will add years to your life. I'm writing out clear directions to Wisdom Way, I'm drawing a map to Righteous Road. I don't want you ending up in blind alleys, or wasting time making wrong turns.*
>
> Proverbs 4:10–12, THE MESSAGE

▼

What do God's promises teach families about finances and possessions?

Financially providing for a family is a constant concern. The cost of living skyrockets and causes you to look for ways to cut back on expenses. But the family has become accustomed to a certain lifestyle and balks at the idea of giving up some pleasure. It seems as if you pay off one debt only to enter into another. Then there are unexpected expenses that wipe out the family savings. Will God's promises help a family manage their finances and possessions?

answer

▼

First, families must realize that God created everything in the world, and it all belongs to Him. Second, they must understand that everyone enters this world without possessions and leaves the same way. Gaining wealth or gathering stuff is not the main purpose of life, and it will never give a family lasting happiness. The family will just want more and more money to buy more and more stuff. "Those who want to be rich fall into temptation and are trapped by many senseless and harmful desires that plunge people into ruin and destruction. For the love of money is a root of all kinds of evil, and in their eagerness to be rich some have wandered away from the faith and pierced themselves with many pains" (1 Timothy 6:9–10, NRSV).

God expects you to work to pay your bills. Money allows you to do two things: live in comfort and help those in need. Families must realize that they are just the caretakers of what God has allowed them to possess. This is often referred to as stewardship, taking care of what God has entrusted to you. Be assured that God is watching to see how a family handles the finances and the possessions He has placed in their care.

worth thinking about

▶ **Life is not** what you have, but who you are. "A sterling reputation is better than striking it rich; a gracious spirit is better than money in the bank" (Proverbs 22:1, THE MESSAGE).

▶ **Guide your** family's focus to those in need. Teach them to give not only physically but also financially from their earnings; otherwise they may only consider their wants and become greedy. "You cannot serve both God and money" (Luke 16:13, NLT).

▶ **Help your** family to recognize where peace and joy come from, not from material things, but from God.

> *Don't store up treasures here on earth, where moths eat them and rust destroys them, and where thieves break in and steal. Store your treasures in heaven, where moths and rust cannot destroy, and thieves do not break in and steal.*
> Matthew 6:19–20, NLT

question

▼

Does God promise to hear and answer prayers?

The Bible gives numerous accounts of God's hearing and answering prayers. Many people attest that it still happens today, that God answers their prayers. Desperate for help, you decide to give prayer a chance, and you pour out your heart to Him. You're trying to believe that God will answer you. But you'd like to know what promises the Scriptures give regarding prayer. Does God promise to hear and answer everyone who prays?

answer

▼

Scriptures are filled with stories about men and women who received answers to prayers. These accounts, which were recorded in the Bible, give you the assurance that He will hear and answer you. God repeatedly told generations throughout the Bible to ask Him for help. Time and again He promised to supply their needs. His promises are still applicable today. God does not favor one person over another; He answers all who seek Him. You can trust His promises, and they will serve as an anchor for your faith.

One man brought his son, who had seizures, to Jesus for healing. The father asked Jesus to help him if He could. When Jesus told the man that all things are possible if you believe, the man replied, "I do have faith, but not enough. Help me have more!" (Mark 9:24, GNT). Believe, but if your faith is experiencing a tremor, do not be afraid to ask God to help you turn from your trembling and trust in His power.

Earthly fathers know how to listen to and answer their children, and God far surpasses them. Human fathers may not give the desired answer, but in most cases their answers will be for the good of their children. They almost always act out of their love. God works on an even grander scale. He loves His children beyond comprehension. He will answer you because He loves and cares about you.

worth thinking about

- ▶ **Look at God's** track record. Read the accounts in the Bible that speak of answered prayer. Talk to people around you; discover that God still answers prayer.

- ▶ **Choose to believe** God hears and will answer. Either you believe God is who He says He is and will do what He says He will, or you do not. You cannot have it both ways.

- ▶ **Understand that God** does not lie. God is holy, without fault. It is not His nature to be untruthful. "You will call to me. You will come and pray to me, and I will answer you" (Jeremiah 29:12, GNT).

Ask and it will be given to you; seek and you will find; knock and the door will be opened to you. For everyone who asks receives; he who seeks finds; and to him who knocks, the door will be opened.

Matthew 7:7–8, NIV

question

Does God promise that prayer may change His heart?

A friend's husband recovered from a serious illness. Another friend underwent a biopsy for cancer, and happily the results showed it was benign. Both claim their successful outcomes were due to prayer. You've always believed in prayer, but you do have questions about it. If God knows everything, including the outcome, why spend time in prayer? Life goes on even if people do not pray. Will prayer change the outcome? Does the Bible shed any light on this matter?

answer

Scripture shows that prayer may change the heart of God. The Old Testament tells of King Hezekiah, who became sick with a life-threatening disease. God sent the prophet Isaiah to advise him to get his affairs in order because Hezekiah was going to die. Hezekiah began to pray earnestly, begging God for his life. God responded by sending Isaiah back to tell him that God said, "I have heard your prayer and seen your tears; I will heal you....I will add fifteen years to your life" (2 Kings 20:5–6, NIV). Hezekiah's life was extended in direct answer to his prayers.

Another biblical example of prayer changing God's heart occurred when Abraham interceded for God's followers who were living in Sodom and Gomorrah. Through prayer, Abraham boldly discussed with God what was to be done and asked Him to spare those who belonged to Him. In the end, Abraham resolved to trust God's final decision. Prayer can change God's heart, and, more important, prayer will change you and enlarge your trust in God's decision.

The stories of Hezekiah and Abraham show that God longs to give you the things you need and want. God promises to hear and answer prayers. He may answer the way you'd like, or He may choose not to grant your request for reasons you do not comprehend. Still, you can trust God because He understands. He sees the complete picture of time and eternity, and He knows how things work together for good.

worth thinking about

- ▶ Prayer is openly and honestly sharing your heart with God, as He shares with you. God is fair, and He promises to listen. Prayer will influence His decision.

- ▶ Prayer—discussing your concerns with God—will change your perception of the situation. He will broaden your understanding of all that is involved. He will enable you to have faith in His decision.

- ▶ Prayer carries you and those you care about through trials and trouble. It is your hope, your assurance, and your guarantee that God will act in your best interest.

> *Trust GOD from the bottom of your heart;*
> *don't try to figure out everything on your own.*
> Proverbs 3:5, THE MESSAGE

question

Why would God promise to answer your prayers?

Many people suggest that prayer should be a way of life and that all decisions should be made with prayer. The way you see it, God has bigger things to tend to than your daily needs. World hunger and war would top the list. Does God have a rank-and-order system that He uses when answering prayer? If so, you'd be way down the list, since you're just an ordinary person. You know that you would surely be at the end of His line.

answer

You are special to God because He created you in His image. And because you are His child, He will answer your prayers. His great love for you is evident by the fact that He sent His Son into the world for your benefit. "God showed how much he loved us by having Christ die for us, even though we were sinful" (Romans 5:8, CEV). Think about that. God's love is obvious, when you consider that He sent His only Son to die for you so you can spend eternity in heaven. Focusing on God's gift can erase all doubts that you might not be important to Him.

God is busy tending to the world and everything in it, but He is so mighty that He can do that and take care of you, too. Due to the limits of the human mind, it is impossible to comprehend the total power and greatness of God. Jesus taught this: "Are not two sparrows sold for a penny? Yet not one of them will fall to the ground apart from the will of your Father. And even the very hairs of your head are all numbered. So don't be afraid; you are worth more than many sparrows" (Matthew 10:29–31, NIV). If God knows the number of hairs on your head, surely you are important enough for Him to listen to your prayers. No one is ahead of you in God's prayer line. He will hear your prayers.

worth thinking about

▶ **Respect yourself** as God's creation. Because of your value, He will answer your prayers.

▶ **Remember that** God's love is unconditional. It is not dependent on what you do or do not do. "By the free gift of God's grace all are put right with him through Christ Jesus, who sets them free" (Romans 3:24, GNT). God is a giver, and He will freely give you answers.

▶ **Recognize the power** of God. God made heaven and earth, and nothing is too hard for Him. God has the power to answer your prayers.

> *When I look at your heavens, the work of your fingers, the moon and the stars that you have established; what are human beings that you are mindful of them, mortals that you care for them? Yet you have made them a little lower than God, and crowned them with glory and honor.*
>
> Psalm 8:3–5, NRSV

54

question

Does God promise an immediate answer to prayer?

Friends have been praying about a particular matter for years without any sign of an answer. The Scriptures promise that God hears, so is He ignoring their request? Surely God realizes all that is at stake and sees how desperately the situation needs to be resolved. Some people advise them to keep on praying and tell them that God will eventually answer. Has God answered by saying no, or is He saying not yet? Does God have a promise that explains the waiting?

answer

God always hears your prayers and answers. His answer may not be what you desired. "'My thoughts are not your thoughts, neither are your ways my ways,' declares the LORD. 'As the heavens are higher than the earth, so are my ways higher than your ways and my thoughts than your thoughts'" (Isaiah 55:8–9, NIV). God may answer yes, no, or not yet. When God says no, He directs you another way or makes another answer obvious. It is when nothing seems to happen that God is saying, "Wait upon My timing." This is the time you must cling to God's promise that He hears and answers prayer. The tighter you hold to the promise, the easier it will be to wait.

You may make a request for a friend or family member, but God's answer may involve several lives. You are definitely eager for the answer, but the person you have prayed for may not be ready. Perhaps God is in the process of healing him of a deep hurt, or is changing his heart. Maybe the answer will affect an entire family, and God is preparing everyone. Like a puzzle, when all the pieces fit together the picture will be complete and the answer will come. "This vision is for a future time. It describes the end, and it will be fulfilled. If it seems slow in coming, wait patiently, for it will surely take place. It will not be delayed" (Habakkuk 2:3, NLT).

worth thinking about

▶ **God promises to answer** even when a situation has to be slowly resolved. Picture several strands of yarn entangled. One by one the knots are worked out and the skeins rewound. God often works on several intertwined lives until at last He brings restoration to all involved.

▶ **God promises to hear** your prayers and heal your wounds. Deep physical wounds take longer to heal than surface wounds. The same is true regarding deep spiritual wounds: time is needed.

▶ **The answer** is promised, but it may not happen quickly. The secret to the waiting is in the believing.

> *As for me, I watch in hope for the LORD, I wait for God my Savior; my God will hear me.*
> Micah 7:7, NIV

55

What is God's promise if you persist in prayer?

Months have passed, and there is still no answer to your prayer. Should you keep asking God, or are you supposed to assume He heard you the first time and will answer? One of your friends said it shows trust if you quit bugging God. Another has told you to persist. How are you to know which is right? It is all very confusing. Does the Bible give any guidance or promises about persisting in prayer?

answer
▼

The story of Hannah can be found in the Book of 1 Samuel in the Old Testament. Hannah wanted a child and continued to bring her request before God. Hannah's persistence was rewarded with a son, Samuel.

The New Testament continues to encourage you to persist in prayer. Jesus told the story of a woman and a judge. The woman kept pleading with the judge to help her, but he refused to do anything. Still, the woman kept asking. Finally he helped her so she would leave him alone. Jesus continued, "Do you hear what that judge, corrupt as he is, is saying? So what makes you think God won't step in and work justice for his chosen people, who continue to cry out for help? Won't he stick up for them? I assure you, he will" (Luke 18:6–8, THE MESSAGE).

Jesus teaches that you are to persist in prayer. Trust that He has heard your requests and is working to bring it about. Believe that He is working behind the scenes, and thank Him for it. Thank Him for what He is doing at the moment you pray and for how He will answer in the future.

Persistence confirms to God how much value you place on the request. When you go to Him daily, He knows that your request is important to you.

worth thinking about

▶ **Jesus made** a point of teaching that persistence in prayer would eventually result in receiving the answer from God. God keeps His promises. Persistence pays off.

▶ **Persistent prayer** reveals to God your level of trust in Him. Your prayer shows that you are confident of His promised answer.

▶ **Scripture teaches** that God desires to give good things to His children. Persistent prayer indicates to God that you recognize Him as your heavenly Father and that you believe in His goodness.

> *Morning, noon, and night I cry out in my distress, and the LORD hears my voice.*
> Psalm 55:17, NLT

Does God do only what we ask?

To him who is able to do immeasurably more than all we ask or imagine, according to his power that is at work within us, to him be glory in the church and in Christ Jesus throughout all generations, for ever and ever! Amen.

Ephesians 3:20–21, NIV

56 question

Does God promise to answer in times of trouble?

Life is threatening to unravel. Numerous problems are pulling you one way and then another. Only God could help you keep it together, but you hesitate to ask. You've always tried to manage on your own and not bother anyone, not even God, with your problems. Because you haven't prayed during the good times, you wonder if He will listen to you in your time of trouble. What does the Bible have to say about this? Is it okay to turn to Him now?

answer

When you come to the end of yourself, realizing that you do not have the answers, God will be waiting for you. Deuteronomy 4 teaches that when you seek God, you will find Him. God promises He will be there. He will be full of kindness toward you and will help you if you sincerely ask Him to. "Ask, and you will receive. Search, and you will find. Knock, and the door will be opened for you. Everyone who asks will receive. Everyone who searches will find. And the door will be opened for everyone who knocks" (Matthew 7:7–8, cev). God promises to answer.

Recognize God's authority and power as the Creator. The Bible speaks of an officer who asked Jesus to heal his servant. Jesus agreed and offered to go to his home. "'Oh no, sir,' answered the officer. 'I do not deserve to have you come into my house. Just give the order, and my servant will get well'" (Matthew 8:8, GNT). The officer realized the power of God. He realized that Jesus could speak the word and the servant would be healed.

Trouble comes to all, but those who seek God and follow Him can be sure of God's promise. He will be with them. Jesus told His disciples, "Here on earth you will have many trials and sorrows. But take heart, because I have overcome the world" (John 16:33, NLT).

worth thinking about

▶ **Seek God** and receive His promised cover of protection. He gives you shelter from the cares that beat you down.

▶ **When you are** sick, you go to the doctor. You take the professional's advice and make changes in your lifestyle. When spiritually sick, go to God. God's promises provide spiritual health.

▶ **God placed** you in a family, not only for physical nurturing, but also for the protective power that someone more capable can provide. God allows you to learn how power and authority work, so that you can wisely trust His promises.

> *Though I walk in the midst of trouble, you preserve me against the wrath of my enemies; you stretch out your hand, and your right hand delivers me.*
> Psalm 138:7, NRSV

question

Is it important to believe God promises to answer prayers?

God is able to answer prayers. Yet sometimes you struggle to believe that He will answer in the way you hope. Does God understand your struggle with doubts? Can you trust God for the best possible answer, knowing it may not be the one you would choose? How important is it to believe that you'll get the hoped-for results? Does believing have anything to do with His answer? Is trust a guarantee that everything will turn out okay?

answer

Scripture refers to your belief and hope in an unseen God as faith. "Faith is being sure of what we hope for and certain of what we do not see" (Hebrews 11:1, NIV). Jesus' brief ministry on earth was a special time in history when miraculous healings occurred in rapid succession. The numerous miracles recorded in the first four books of the New Testament—Matthew, Mark, Luke, and John— glorified God and substantiated that Jesus was God's Son.

Miracles are still happening, but it may not always appear that way to the human mind. God in heaven sees the complete picture of your time on earth. You may never understand God's miraculous answers until you get to heaven. But you can trust that His decision will be the wisest one.

The apostle James stressed the importance of asking for wisdom when going through trials. "When you pray, you must believe and not doubt at all. Whoever doubts is like a wave in the sea that is driven and blown about by the wind" (James 1:6, GNT). James did not mean that if you just believe enough, you will have the answer you desire. Instead, he was saying that when you are in the midst of a trial, believe; have faith that God is at work and will get you through it. Do not doubt God's ability to answer or His decision regarding your request.

worth thinking about

▶ **God grants** the gift of faith in Him, but some people never open the package. You will realize how large His gift of faith is when you start to believe.

▶ **God's answers** build your faith. His promises can get you through trials, while doubts will destroy your hope. God will help you overcome doubt by filling you with His promises.

▶ **Trust God's** wisdom over yours. Tell God the answer you desire, but seek and trust His will for the best possible outcome.

How bold and free we then become in his presence, freely asking according to his will, sure that he's listening. And if we're confident that he's listening, we know that what we've asked for is as good as ours.
1 John 5:14–15, THE MESSAGE

question

Does God promise to answer when wrongs are confessed?

Regret is not a new word to you. You definitely have experienced it: words that you wish you could take back, thoughts that were downright cruel, and other things you'd rather not mention. Recently you heard that not telling God about your wrongdoing could block answers to prayer. Why do you need to specifically tell God the things you've done that go against His laws? Doesn't He already know, and hasn't Jesus already forgiven you?

answer

God knows all about you. There is nowhere you can go to escape His presence. God knows the good things you've done as well as the times you've broken His law. "Sin is the same as breaking God's law" (1 John 3:4, CEV). When you choose Jesus to be Lord of your life, all the things you have done that displease God—past, present, and future—are forgiven. God dislikes the breaking of His laws, but He loves you. Jesus came to save people from the consequences of their wrong actions. "There is therefore now no condemnation for those who are in Christ Jesus. For the law of the Spirit of life in Christ Jesus has set you free from the law of sin and of death" (Romans 8:1–2, NRSV).

Talk to God about the things you have done that dis-pleased Him. He wants you to agree with Him that break-ing His laws is wrong and brings harm to you and others. When you realize that, you are ready to turn to a better way of life. God and you will be on the same page! Confess, so that the answers to your prayers will not be delayed. The psalmist wrote: "If I had not confessed the sin in my heart, the Lord would not have listened" (Psalm 66:18, NLT). Confession is necessary to show God that you agree with Him. God promises forgiveness to those who seek Him and confess their faults.

worth thinking about

- ▶ **God does not** ask you to confess so you can receive punishment. He already knows and can bring your wrong to light without your help. God's desire is for you to tell Him and to agree with Him that it was wrong. He wants you to confess so you can be freed from your guilt.

- ▶ **Dirt in a drainage** pipe blocks the flow. Wrongs that are not confessed block the spiritual flow between you and God.

- ▶ **Confessing your wrongs** to God gets rid of the static in your spiritual connection. God's answers to your prayers will flow freely.

> *Generous in love—God, give grace! Huge in mercy—wipe out my bad record. Scrub away my guilt, soak out my sins in your laundry. I know how bad I've been; my sins are staring me down. . . . What you're after is truth from the inside out.*
> Psalm 51:1–3, 6, THE MESSAGE

59 question

Does God promise to forgive and not condemn?

People say that God is a God of forgiveness and not a God of condemnation. That's hard for you to grasp, for you know that God is perfect and has no faults. You've always heard that breaking God's laws results in punishment. Surely He will have to come down hard on you for some of your mistakes. Your life has been filled with one ugly mess after another. You cannot even forgive yourself, so how could God forgive you? Won't He condemn you?

answer

God sent His Son to earth to pay for your wrongs. "If you belong to Christ Jesus, you won't be punished" (Romans 8:1, CEV). This is good news! There is no condemnation, just forgiveness for those who stand with Jesus. When God looks at you, He does not see your wrongdoing. He just sees Jesus' goodness instead of your past. Your wrongs are wiped away, and your life is cleared of all those times you displeased God by breaking His laws. You can begin again. God's forgiveness is a gift of grace—something you cannot earn. It is not a result of anything you do.

When God forgives, the Bible says that "he has removed our sins s far from us as the east is from the west" (Psalm 103:12, NLT). If you try to bring up a past mistake, God does not know what you are talking about. If God says you're okay, then forgive yourself. His love is powerful. Leave your past mistakes with Him. Do not keep dragging around your regrets.

God may point out that you need to change in some area of your life, but He will do it in an encouraging way, guiding your heart and mind by His Spirit. Satan, the evil one, will nag at you with doubts and use accusations to make you feel unworthy. As long as you feel like pond scum, you will not be able to tell others about God.

worth thinking about

▶ The first four books of the New Testament—Matthew, Mark, Luke, and John—are called Gospels. *Gospel* means "good news." These books are filled with the promises of good news: Jesus took your punishment and freed you from your failures.

▶ God does not keep reminding you of past mistakes. He promises to forgive and forget. God tells you how to follow His laws and live a better life.

▶ Accepting God's forgiveness and putting your past behind you is saying yes to His gift of grace and showing that you believe He really did die in your place.

It's urgent that you listen carefully to this: Anyone here who believes what I am saying right now and aligns himself with the Father, who has in fact put me in charge, has at this very moment the real, lasting life and is no longer condemned to be an outsider.

John 5:24, The Message

60

Does God promise to hear your prayer for personal help?

Praying for others and for the world seems like the right thing to do. Yet you've never been quite sure if it is all right to pray for yourself. It seems like a self-centered thing to do. But the other day, a friend commented that she prays for herself. When you expressed surprise, she explained that she needs God's strength. She said that she wouldn't be able to do half of what she does without His help. Is it okay to pray for yourself?

answer

God makes this simple to understand when He says He is your heavenly Father and invites you to bring your concerns to Him as His child. He intends for you to openly discuss your personal needs and the needs of others with Him in prayer. Many biblical characters claimed God as a close confidant. God shared His plans with them in prayer. His close relationship with them shows you His desire to know you personally.

The Book of Psalms is filled with prayers. If you take your cue from David, who wrote many of the psalms, you are to let God know your personal needs. David prayed for protection. "Listen, GOD! Please, pay attention! Can you make sense of these ramblings, my groans and cries? King-

God, I need your help" (Psalm 5:1-2, THE MESSAGE). He prayed when he was depressed, "My God, my God, why have you abandoned me? I have cried desperately for help, but still it does not come" (Psalm 22:1, GNT). He prayed in times of happiness. "I bless GOD every chance I get; my lungs expand with his praise" (Psalm 34:1, THE MESSAGE).

Feelings that tell you not to seek God's help for your needs are just that. Feelings. They do not come from God. The Bible is God's truth. It guides you to turn to Him. God is interested in everything that concerns you, and He promises to answer your personal prayers.

worth thinking about

▶ **Tell God** your need. When you ask God to help you, you are affirming that you believe His promises—that He desires you to call on Him, and that He has the power to help you.

▶ **Thank God** for His answer before it even comes to pass. He promises to supply your needs.

▶ **Trust God** while you wait. Sometimes, it may take a while for things to come together, but He does promise that He will bring it to pass.

> *Don't fret or worry. Instead of worrying, pray. Let petitions and praises shape your worries into prayers, letting God know your concerns. Before you know it, a sense of God's wholeness, everything coming together for good, will come and settle you down.*
> Philippians 4:6–7, THE MESSAGE

61

question

What does God promise when you are stressed to the max?

Trying to juggle family, home, and work is getting to you. A notice in the mail reminded you about an overdue bill. It happened only because you didn't have time to write out the payment. There is no way to accomplish everything unless you give up sleep. God might be able to help you make sense of your life, but you haven't had time for Him in way too many months. How can God help you? Does He have a remedy for stress?

answer

God showed you how important rest is when He rested on the seventh day after creation. Your body was not designed to go-go-go without renewing it with sleep. "I lay down and slept, yet I woke up in safety, for the LORD was watching over me" (Psalm 3:5, NLT). God gives sleep to refresh. It is only when your life gets out of balance physically, spiritually, or emotionally that you start dropping the juggling pins of life. If you look at Jesus' life, you can get a clue as to how to keep it in balance.

Jesus kept an extremely busy schedule during His time on earth. He was always teaching or healing. Yet when He grew weary, He always slipped away to pray. He sent His disciples on ahead after preaching and feeding a crowd of more than five thousand. "After sending them home, he went up into the hills by himself to pray" (Matthew 14:23, NLT). Jesus knew how important it was to spend some one-on-one time with God the Father. He was refueling and refreshing His Spirit.

Busyness can cause life to begin a downward spiral, where important values are lost. Spending time with God in prayer can be an anchor that keeps you grounded. Jesus said, "Come to me, all of you who are weary and carry heavy burdens, and I will give you rest. Take my yoke upon you. Let me teach you, because I am humble and gentle at heart, and you will find rest for your souls" (Matthew 11:28–29, NLT).

worth thinking about

▶ **Take a break.** The prophet Elijah was stressed to the max (1 Kings 19). He needed to get away from everything. God refreshed him with rest and food.

▶ **Talk it over** with God. Elijah told God exactly how he felt about everything. He trusted God to accept his feelings, and God spoke to him in a gentle voice.

▶ **Thank God** for His help and support. God chose the prophet Elisha to help Elijah. God provided some assistance, and Elisha continued the work after Elijah.

> *Those who trust the LORD will find new strength. They will be strong like eagles soaring upward on wings; they will walk and run without getting tired.*
> Isaiah 40:31, CEV

62 question
▼

How can God promise you peace when you feel confused?

You've never felt more confused in your entire life. All avenues of your life seem to have a Road Closed or Detour sign posted. What are you to do when your way is blocked? You do not like to wait, and detour signs are just as bad. What if you lose your way? You like to know exactly how things are supposed to go. Your anxiety level is about to max out. Does God promise peace in the midst of confusion?

answer
▼

When all roads are impassable, God does give you a way to reassurance and peace while you wait. "There are some things that the LORD our God has kept secret; but he has revealed his Law, and we and our descendants are to obey it forever" (Deuteronomy 29:29, GNT). You may not understand the why of your situation, but God does. He is in control. In these times of confusion, He desires for you to remember how He has worked in your life or others' lives in the past. Remembering His past faithfulness is what will give you the confidence to trust Him.

People in biblical times were instructed by God to remember all that He had done for them. They were to talk about these stories and share them with their children. "We will not hide these truths from our children; we will tell the next generation about the glorious deeds of the LORD, about his power and his mighty wonders" (Psalm 78:4, NLT). God was not into having a brag session. His purpose for the recounting of past events was for the benefit of His children. Going over the past miracles reminded them that they served a God who could be trusted. When you think back to how God has worked in your life, or look at how He has helped someone else, you are reassured. God is a mighty God who works on behalf of His people. God's promise of peace will route confusion away from you.

worth thinking about

▶ **Light illuminates** the way. You do not have to have the entire path lit at once. God gives you enough light to take the next step. "O LORD, you give me light; you dispel my darkness" (Psalm 18:28, GNT).

▶ **Trust eliminates** confusion. "Some trust in their war chariots and others in their horses, but we trust in the power of the LORD our God" (Psalm 20:7, GNT).

▶ **Hope rejuvenates** your spirit. Confusion turns to peace when you stir up your hope in God by remembering all He has done.

> *You will keep in perfect peace all who trust in you, all whose thoughts are fixed on you! Trust in the LORD always, for the LORD GOD is the eternal Rock.*
> Isaiah 26:3–4, NLT

question
▼
Where is God's promised peace in a war-torn world?

War seems to be ongoing; if it is not this war, then it is another. Families are torn apart by separation and even some by death. Everyone has an opinion about what should be done. In the news, you hear of other places all around the world that are threatening war action. You figure if one war ends, another will just erupt. You want the fighting to stop and peace to return. After all, how can you have peace in a war-torn world?

answer
▼

Satan took the form of a serpent and tempted Adam and Eve in the Garden of Eden. Because they accepted the serpent's temptation and disobeyed God, evil entered the world. There cannot be a physical peace while good and evil exist together on this earth. The peace God promises in a war-torn world is an inner peace, which His Spirit—often referred to as the Holy Spirit—gives to you. The secret to finding that type of peace is in trusting God in every situation, and His Spirit will help you do it. Believe God is still on His throne, and He is in control.

Jesus prepared His followers for the time He would return to heaven. He warned them about things that would happen in this world: "When reports come in of wars and rumored wars, keep your head and don't panic. This is routine history; this is no sign of the end" (Matthew 24:6, THE MESSAGE). He knew the idea of war and battles raging continually would fill them with trepidation. That is why He promised to send the Holy Spirit to live in their hearts. Your path to peace during this time of trouble is to believe God's promises, pray for those who are suffering, and stay close to God.

God wants you to stay connected to Him so His peace can flow through you even in times like war. Your faith in God will enable His Spirit to calm your anxiety as you trust Him more and more.

worth thinking about

▶ **Prayer gives** inner peace as you realize He promises to answer and rescue you from trouble. Scripture says that the promised Holy Spirit prays within you as you pray.

▶ **God's promises** bring inner peace. Make a list of them and read them over and over.

▶ **Exercising your trust** produces inner peace. Act and speak words that show you trust God in the circumstances. Refuse negative thoughts and words by refusing to speak or think them. God can do anything, and His promised Spirit lives within you.

I'm leaving you well and whole. That's my parting gift to you. Peace. I don't leave you the way you're used to being left—feeling abandoned, bereft. So don't be upset. Don't be distraught.

John 14:27, THE MESSAGE

question

▾

What promises does God give for overcoming anxiety?

Anxiety is that nagging feeling that something is not right. You can never put your finger on the exact cause. The surface of your mind must be like sticky tape, and every little worry adheres. Sometimes anxiety almost makes you panic. Its constant presence won't let you rest, at least not for long. You'd give anything just to be able to let go of all your cares and feel at peace. What promises does God give for overcoming anxiety?

answer

▾

It is God's desire that you feel His peace. David wrote in one of his psalms, "Pile your troubles on GOD's shoulders—he'll carry your load, he'll help you out" (Psalm 55:22, THE MESSAGE). David trusted God with all of his worries. He knew God was on his side. The Bible teaches that God loves you; God is in control; and God is all-powerful. Let those facts penetrate your mind. Stop the worry habit, and start the trust habit.

Jesus emphasized that worry was not in God's plan for you. He repeatedly stressed this truth: "I tell you not to worry about your life. Don't worry about having something to eat, drink, or wear. Isn't life more than food or clothing? . . . Can worry make you live longer? . . .

Don't worry about tomorrow. It will take care of itself. You have enough to worry about today" (Matthew 6:25, 27, 34, CEV).

Psychologists say that it is impossible for the human mind to think two thoughts at the same time. You cannot think of God and your fears simultaneously. God did give you some direction on what you are to think about. "Whatever is true, whatever is noble, . . . whatever is lovely, whatever is admirable—if anything is excellent or praiseworthy—think about such things" (Philippians 4:8, NIV). You are to reject anxious thoughts and find positive things to think on. God promises that trusting Him—thinking His thoughts—will overcome anxious thoughts.

worth thinking about

▶ **Renew your thinking.** Trade negative thinking for positive thinking. Negative thinking does not come from God. Reject it. God has given you a strong mind, and you can learn to think God thoughts!

▶ **Rejoice, thanking God** for everything. Each day tell God thank You for what He does for you. Make gratitude your attitude.

▶ **Rest in His arms** of love. Say good-bye to anxiety about the past. You cannot change it. Say good-bye to worries about the present. God is in charge. Say good-bye to fears about the future. God is your protector.

> *To set the mind on the flesh is death, but to set the mind on the Spirit is life and peace.*
> Romans 8:6, NRSV

question

Does God promise peace in the midst of turmoil at work?

The workplace is great when everyone is getting along, but when they're not, it is the pits. Two people are no longer speaking. The argument was about a possible promotion and pay raise. If you had your way, you'd eat your lunch in the peace of your office so you wouldn't have to listen to any of it. No matter how it goes, it is going to be a while before the air clears. Will God help you find peace in the midst of this squabble?

answer

Jesus spent His ministry teaching people how to live. Jesus said that you can be like a light in a darkened world by shining with His love, or like salt, seasoning people with His peace. God values peace, for Jesus taught, "Blessed are the peacemakers, for they will be called sons of God" (Matthew 5:9, NIV). You are called to live in peace.

Friction at work provides the perfect opportunity to put into practice some of the teachings of Jesus. "Watch the way you talk. Let nothing foul or dirty come out of your mouth. Say only what helps, each word a gift. . . . Make a clean break with all cutting, backbiting, profane talk. Be gentle with one another, sensitive. Forgive one another as quickly and thoroughly as God in Christ forgave you" (Ephesians 4:29, 32, THE MESSAGE).

Disagreements will always be a part of life. It is how you disagree that defines your character. Choosing words of peace does not mean that you have to be noncommittal; you can give an opinion without tearing someone apart with your words. Do it God's way: be a peacemaker by refusing to use negative words. Stay clear of backbiting and gossip. Steer conversations to subjects and comments that encourage others. If someone hurts you with unkind comments, set the example by forgiving them. God will bless you with His peace.

worth thinking about

▶ **Speak the language** of peace. Refuse to be drawn into arguments or gossip sessions. Learn to control your words and receive God's promised blessing for peacemakers.

▶ **Season the workplace** with acts of kindness. Every action produces another like it. Ignore irritations and spread goodwill. The promise of peace will result.

▶ **Seek His peace.** Learn about God. "Take my yoke and put it on you, and learn from me, because I am gentle and humble in spirit; and you will find rest" (Matthew 11:29, GNT).

> *Try to live at peace with everyone! Live a clean life. If you don't, you will never see the Lord. Make sure that no one misses out on God's wonderful kindness. Don't let anyone become bitter and cause trouble for the rest of you.*
>
> Hebrews 12:14–15, CEV

question

question

How can anyone find peace?

answer

He himself is our peace, who has made the two one and has destroyed the barrier, the dividing wall of hostility, by abolishing in his flesh the law with its command- ments and regulations.

Ephesians 2:14–15, NIV

66

question

What are God's promises for overcoming disappointment?

God's handwriting seemed to be all over a promising opportunity, but it fell through. If God is in control, why did He let you think it was going to work out? Now you feel like giving up and never trying again. What does God want you to do? What is His promise for surviving shattered dreams? How do you pick up the pieces and go on? Does the Bible give any promises for climbing up from the valley of disappointment?

answer

God may have delayed the fulfillment of your dream, or He may have a better one waiting for you around the corner. This much you can know from God's teachings: He is on your side. "What then are we to say about these things? If God is for us, who is against us? He who did not withhold his own Son, but gave him up for all of us, will he not with him also give us everything else?" (Romans 8:31–32, NRSV). God has promised you His best. Will you trust Him for the next good thing? Trusting that God knows best is the ladder on which you can climb out of the valley of disappointment. He knows what's in your future and what other good things lay ahead.

Pull up any root of bitterness that starts to grow in your heart or mind. Instead, keep your eyes upon God. Peter was a disciple of Jesus. When he kept his eyes on Jesus, Peter could do the impossible. In fact, he started to walk on the water like Jesus. But when Peter took his eyes off Jesus and looked at the threatening storm, he sank. Jesus immediately reached out and caught him. Peter's situation helps you understand how important it is to keep your focus on God. But if you do start to sink, know that Jesus will lift you up.

worth thinking about

- ▶ **Climb up with** trust. Disappointments are only a part of life, not all of it. Trust God's promise that He is for you, not against you.

- ▶ **Take three more** steps up. "Be joyful in hope, patient in affliction, faithful in prayer" (Romans 12:12, NIV).

- ▶ **You're at the** top when you trust God in spite of your circumstances. If you never experienced the valley of disappointment, you'd never know the height of God's promised goodness.

> *Keep your eyes on Jesus, who both began and finished this race we're in. Study how he did it. Because he never lost sight of where he was headed—that exhilarating finish in and with God—he could put up with anything along the way: cross, shame, whatever.*
>
> Hebrew 12:2, THE MESSAGE

question

What is God's promised peace for family problems?

Family concerns—is there no escaping them? Sickness, financial worries, and relational problems beat on your family's door continually. How are you supposed to feel peace when someone in your extended family is always in crisis? There is always someone to worry about, and generally there are several at once. You feel weighted down with all the cares. You'd like to escape from the stresses, but you know it is not possible. Does God promise peace in spite of such worries?

answer

Jesus talked with His disciples about why there is pain and suffering in the world. The Bible teaches that evil made its entry into the world when the first man and first woman broke God's unconditional covenant. Since that time, and until Jesus' return, good and evil must exist side by side. The result is that all lives are touched by sorrow and pain.

The good news is that God has promised to give you a peace that is from heaven. When the world says peace, it means a moment brought about by a happy circumstance. But God's peace comes from knowing His promises are yours. His promises become yours when you accept what He did for you. He took your punishment for breaking

God's laws and gave His life in your place. Now you can believe God's promises and spend eternity in heaven.

When those closest to you are experiencing pain and sorrow, your heart aches for them. Realize you cannot fix it. Only God can, and He will, for He alone knows what is needed in their lives. Trust Him to draw them closer to Him during their time of suffering. He is working in them as well as in you.

Jesus never gave the illusion that once you chose to follow Him life would be perfect. There will still be various types of family problems, but you can give your concerns to Him in prayer. He promises to answer and will be with you as you go through each situation.

worth thinking about

▶ **Think on God's** truth—He's the winner over evil. Your emotions, damaged by all your trials and troubles, tell you everything is lost. God's truth is that He's already won the battle!

▶ **Surrender each day's** cares to God. There are no problems that are too big for God.

▶ **Trust, for He** is watching over you and yours. God never sleeps, and He is all-knowing. He will not take His eye off of you.

> *Sing for joy, O heavens, and exult, O earth; break forth, O mountains, into singing! For the LORD has comforted his people, and will have compassion on his suffering ones.*
>
> Isaiah 49:13, NRSV

question

What peace does God promise when you're lonely?

Loneliness is tough, and almost everyone has experienced it at some point or another. It can be a physical loneliness, or it can be an emotional one. Regardless of the type, you just know you feel alone. You may try to escape it by turning on music or the TV for companionship. You may seek the company of others, only to discover that gives no relief. What is God's promised comfort for loneliness? Does He offer you any peace?

answer

God never intends for anyone to feel alone; He created you for a relationship with Him. Scripture says He delights in you and desires that you draw near to Him. In response, He will draw near to you and make you aware of His presence. "The Lord has promised that he will not leave us or desert us" (Hebrews 13:5, CEV). God never breaks a promise.

Your life on earth is in a constant cycle of change. You are born into a family, and then you leave your childhood home to establish new relationships and homes. There are times you will be physically alone, and there will be times when you will feel emotionally alone. But you are never alone if you draw near to God.

Jesus told His disciples that He would die and would then rise again on the third day after His death. He would return to heaven shortly thereafter. They struggled to understand and they were worried about being left alone. Jesus assured them that they wouldn't be. He promised that after He returned to heaven He would send His Spirit to live in the hearts of all who put their trust in God. Jesus did as He promised. God's Holy Spirit lives within you when you trust God. The feeling of being alone is just that, a feeling. The truth is you are never alone, for wherever you are, God's Spirit is within you.

worth thinking about

▶ Tell the lonely feelings to scat; they are false, and you are never alone. Psalm 139 says that it is impossible to flee from God's presence.

▶ Affirm God's truth; He is with you. The Scriptures tell you that He is with you in the daytime and is with you in the night. He will never leave you.

▶ Acknowledge God's presence by speaking to Him in prayer. Read the Psalms, and believe His promises.

> Can a woman forget her own baby and not love the child she bore? Even if a mother should forget her child, I will never forget you. . . . I have written your name on the Palms of my hands.
>
> Isaiah 49:15–16, GNT

question

▼

What is God's promised peace when you have to relocate?

When a job promotion requires you to relocate, you know you are in for another major change. It is wonderful to see the world and experience new places, but it is sad to leave your friends. Building new friendships is not always easy. Add to that the stress of finding an affordable house, selling yours, and moving halfway across the country. You long to put down roots, but life today is mobile. How can there be any peace when you're always on the move?

answer

▼

Asking God to guide you to the right neighborhood and home is the first step of wisdom. You can also pray that God will send the person He wants to buy your current home. It is important to include God in the planning of your new home, for "unless the LORD builds the house, those who build it labor in vain" (Psalm 127:1, NRSV). This verse is not talking about just the physical construction, but the establishing of a home on God's principles or rules for living.

Pray about your concern for leaving old friends and making new. Keep in mind that God has a plan for your life. "I know the plans I have for you, says the LORD, plans for your welfare and not for harm, to give you a future with hope" (Jeremiah 29:11, NRSV). Scripture encourages you to give all of your worries to God, for He can handle them. God does not want you weighed down with a bundle of concerns. Worry is the opposite of faith. Stop the worry action!

Start the faith action. Realize that God is everywhere at the same time. He is capable of taking care of the physical details regarding the buying and selling of property, and He is capable of giving you wonderful new friends. He promises you peace when you trust Him.

worth thinking about

▶ **Technology has given** you many ways to stay connected with faraway family and friends through e-mail, cell phones, and landlines. God promises to bless your life. He will enable you to preserve former friendships as well as make new ones.

▶ **Travel makes visits** possible. Airlines can deliver you to your destination within hours. Cars and motor homes make travel leisurely and comfortable. God's promised blessings are everywhere.

▶ **The reality is,** you are always God-connected. The same sun, moon, and stars are shining down on everyone. The same sky covers all, uniting them, though apart.

> *Homes are built on the foundation of wisdom and understanding. Where there is knowledge, the rooms are furnished with valuable, beautiful things.*
>
> Proverbs 24:3-4, GNT

question

Does God promise peace to the caregiver?

Caregiving requires you to be on duty 24-7. There is little rest, and for this period of time, this is your life. You do it out of love, but at times your patience wears thin. You wouldn't have it any other way. But the truth is, you would treasure getting out and doing something relaxing, even going for a walk. Will God renew your strength and keep you going? Will He give you peace?

answer

God commands you to care for the aged and widows in your earthly family and in your church families. "Do not speak harshly to an older man, but speak to him as to a father. . . . If a widow has children or grandchildren, they should first learn their religious duty to their own family and make some repayment to their parents; for this is pleasing in God's sight" (1 Timothy 5:1, 4, NRSV). The Bible gives examples of those who cared for their aging parents. Joseph cared for his father, Jacob, and Ruth cared for her mother-in-law, Naomi. God's promised blessings were evident in both their lives.

God's promised peace comes not only through providing care and being obedient, but it comes also through staying connected to Him. When you are providing care from a heart of love, peace will flow. Stress comes when you are tired and you begin to react out of duty. This is the time to pull aside and talk to God, asking Him to refill you with His love.

Apart from God you will not have the energy or the wisdom to do what has to be done. The Bible teaches that when you ask God for strength and energy, He will provide it. He will redeem your time and stretch your minutes. When you ask Him for wisdom, He will supply it. God will enable you to keep on keeping on when you trust in His promises.

worth thinking about

▶ **Treat yourself** to some help with routine chores like mowing the yard, cleaning the car, or doing housework. Moses was a great leader of the Israelites, but his father-in-law showed him that he had to learn to delegate. One person cannot do it all.

▶ **Take a mini-vacation** by taking a walk, meditating, reading a book, or watching a movie. Ask God to help you find a family member or friend who can provide the little breaks that will renew you.

▶ **Trust God** to supply you with strength and wisdom. "God is our shelter and strength, always ready to help in times of trouble" (Psalm 46:1, GNT).

Listen to your father, who gave you life, and don't despise your mother when she is old. . . . So give your father and mother joy! May she who gave you birth be happy.

Proverbs 23:22, 25, NLT

question

What does God promise when you choose to live His way?

Everywhere you look, people are encumbered with problems. You also have your share. A neighbor invited you to church and said that God would bless you, but you are not sure what that means. You assume she is implying that good things would start happening. But a look at your neighbor's life makes you question this. She has multiple concerns in her family, plus she suffers with poor health. How is God blessing her? What are the benefits that God sends when you live His way?

answer

When God led the Israelites out of slavery to the Promised Land, He gave them civil, moral, and spiritual laws. He didn't give the laws to be a dictator, but out of love for them. He clued them in on the blessings that would result from living a good life, and informed them of the consequences that would evolve from living a wrong lifestyle. God didn't force them to obey, but He gave them a choice. He is still giving that choice to His followers today. God's promised blessings will result if you follow His principles for living.

You do not live in an isolated world. Other people's choices will affect you just as your choices affect them.

When the laws of nature are involved, it is more difficult to see God's promised blessing for those who obey. These laws affect the obedient and rebellious person—when a virus attacks, sickness results. If two cars move toward each other at a fast rate of speed, they will crash and people will be hurt. Many catastrophes can occur. The promised blessing for those who choose God's way is still there. God will go with them through their heartaches. He will see them through every tragedy and will even use their sorrow for good. God never abandons those who choose to obey Him. He will bless their lives with good things and reward them with eternal life.

worth thinking about

▶ **God is a protector** and encourager. He sends His angels to help you. He promises to be with you in your trials and does not waste your suffering. He uses it to make you stronger in your spirit.

▶ **God is a winner,** and He makes you one. "No, in all these things we are more than conquerors through him who loved us" (Romans 8:37, NRSV).

▶ **God is wise,** and His promises can be trusted. He gives you directions for right living and promises blessings for your obedience.

> *I am now giving you the choice between life and death, between God's blessing and God's curse, and I call heaven and earth to witness the choice you make. Choose life.*
> Deuteronomy 30:19, GNT

72

question

What does God promise to those who study the Bible?

The only Bible you're familiar with was the one at your grandparents' house. It always looked difficult to read with its tiny print. The use of *thee* and *thou* sounded funny. But the other day you were in a store when some brightly colored books caught your eye. When you took a closer look, you discovered that they were Bibles and that the wording had been updated. You have always thought it might be smart to read the Bible if you could understand it. Would reading the Scriptures help you?

answer

The Bible teaches that wisdom begins with knowing the Scriptures. The Bible was written by men inspired by God and was written in their original languages of Greek, Aramaic, and Hebrew. Since that time, the Scriptures have been translated into many languages and styles. Many translations read as smoothly as a novel.

God gives numerous blessings and promises to those who study the Bible. Among them is the promise that the Holy Spirit will teach you His truth. He promises that your faith will increase as you study, and reading and meditating upon the Scriptures will bless your life.

Paul, a mighty worker for God, wrote to his dear friend Timothy, and it is applicable to you, "All scripture is inspired by God and is useful for teaching, for reproof, for correction, and for training in righteousness" (2 Timothy 3:16, NRSV). The Bible is really a how-to book for living. God, in His great love for you, wanted to spare you a life of trial and error. He included His laws and principles to guide you through life. When you read the biblical stories included in the Old Testament, you learn about God's personality and His interactions with His children. You also learn by observing the mistakes made by those who lived in ages past. They were men and women who had emotions and needs like yours.

worth thinking about

▶ God's laws are valuable. "They are more desirable than gold, even the finest gold. They are sweeter than honey, even honey dripping from the comb" (Psalm 19:10, NLT).

▶ God's principles are a spiritual medicine. "The instructions of the LORD are perfect, reviving the soul. ...The commandments of the LORD are right, bringing joy to the heart" (Psalm 19:7–8, NLT).

▶ The Scriptures are powerful. "The word of God is alive and active, sharper than any double-edged sword. It cuts all the way through, to where soul and spirit meet, to where joints and marrow come together. It judges the desires and thoughts of the heart" (Hebrews 4:12, GNT).

> *The Law of the Lord is a lamp, and its teachings shine brightly. Correction and self-control will lead you through life.*
> Proverbs 6:23, CEV

question

What does God promise if you stay close to Him?

"If you don't walk close, you'll walk cold." You were surprised when your golfing buddy made that comment about following God. When you asked him what he meant, he said that whenever he neglects his Bible reading and forgets to pray, he soon starts skipping church. When that happens, his relationship with God grows cold. He feels that staying close to God makes his life better. What are God's promises if you stay close to Him?

answer

When two people spend time together, they really get to know each other. Quality time is important, but the truth is, the quantity of time gives depth and breadth to relationships. When you draw near to God and ask Him to take control of your life, His Spirit comes to live within you. "The Holy Spirit produces this kind of fruit in our lives: love, joy, peace, patience, kindness, goodness, faithfulness, gentleness, and self-control. There is no law against these things" (Galatians 5:22–23, NLT).

Staying close to God will enable you to let the Holy Spirit remind you of how God wants you to live. But if you distance yourself from Him, you will return to your old nature. He does make your life better, for when you are at odds with His principles, you encounter those things that take away your peace. When you stay close to Him, He promises that the Holy Spirit will help you.

When you stay close to God, there will be evidence of that. You will do good things to help people. The Bible calls this "bearing fruit." Jesus said to imagine God as the gardener of the world, and Himself as the vine. The branches are the people of the world. If a branch produces good things for God and mankind, God prunes it so it produces even more fruit. If the branch does not produce any fruit, God cuts it off. Apart from the vine, fruit cannot be produced.

worth thinking about

▶ **Stay close** to God and experience His power to help you deal with impossible situations in your family, your job, or the world.

▶ **Draw near** to God and discover that God provides you with every good thing in heaven. His spiritual characteristics, such as love, joy, and peace, will be evident in your life.

▶ **Stay connected** to Jesus. He promises that by staying connected, you will experience His blessings in your life and extend His goodness to others. His actions will become your actions.

Submit yourselves therefore to God. Resist the devil, and he will flee from you. Draw near to God, and he will draw near to you.

James 4:7–8, NRSV

question

Does God promise to give you strength?

Life can be physically, mentally, and spiritually draining. There are times you wish for a deep inward strength that would enable you to jump life's high hurdles. Daily challenges tend to wear you down and make you feel like giving in and giving up. You wish you could draw from some deep reservoir that could replenish physical, mental, and spiritual strength. Could God be that reservoir? Does He promise to give you strength?

answer

When you come to the point that you realize you need God's strength, you are in a good place. The Bible quotes God's promise: "My strength comes into its own in your weakness" (2 Corinthians 12:9, THE MESSAGE).

Prayer is a place where God pours His strength into you. David wrote in one of his psalms, "The moment I called out, you stepped in; you made my life large with strength" (Psalm 138:3, THE MESSAGE). All you need to do is ask. Jesus often went alone to pray; He knew prayer was where daily strengthening takes place. God will strengthen you in three ways. He will give you an inner strength that can get you through times of tragedy as well as through daily trials; a physical strength for endurance; and an emotional strength for mental fatigue.

Meditating, or thinking about God's promises, also fortifies you with strength. As you learn more and more about God and how He cares for you, your trust in Him will give you strength to face life one situation at a time and one day at a time. Jesus also spent time with His disciples, who gave Him support. In the same way, joining with other believers will mutually strengthen you both. God promises His strength to you. Prayer, meditation, and meeting with other believers are all different ways to draw His strength to you.

worth thinking about

▶ **God will answer** your prayer for strength. He will give you strength in your inner spirit and help you face the impossible.

▶ **Meditating on God's** promises will give you mental energy and help you deal with daily situations that rob you of your peace.

▶ **God promises strength** for those who trust Him for physical energy. "He gives power to the weak and strength to the powerless" (Isaiah 40:29, NLT).

> *Those who wait for the LORD shall renew their strength, they shall mount up with wings like eagles, they shall run and not be weary, they shall walk and not faint.*
>
> Isaiah 40:31, NRSV

question

When you do not understand God's actions, are His promises trustworthy?

God was leading one way, and then when you started to follow, circumstances changed. Had you totally misunderstood? If so, why didn't God stop you before you made major changes? Now everything in your life is at disaster stage. On top of that, God seems to be silently waiting for you to make the next move. Has God deserted you? Why would He allow this to happen to you? Can you still trust His promises?

answer

God is the same God that created the earth. He is the God of the past, the present, and the future. He is perfect and holy, and He cannot lie. He is your God, too, and He has promised that He will never desert you. Even if you cannot sense His presence, He is with you. This is a time to activate your trust. That's what faith is—believing that He is there even when you cannot see Him.

Scripture teaches that "Jesus Christ is the same yesterday and today and forever" (Hebrews 13:8, NRSV). It also teaches that to know Jesus is to know God the Father, for Jesus and the Father are One. If Jesus never changes, neither does God. God was faithful to those who lived in biblical times, and He will be faithful to you. You can trust Him, even when you do not understand what He is doing.

'"My thoughts,' says the LORD, 'are not like yours, and my ways are different from yours'" (Isaiah 55:8, GNT). This period of confusion and waiting could be happening for many different reasons, and you may never understand until you get to heaven. But God is in control. He sees the whole puzzle of life, and His Word promises that you can trust Him. He is allowing this disconcerting time and will use it to grow your faith in Him.

worth thinking about

▶ **Faith is a product** of your beliefs. You trust in God's promises because you have reliable evidence in the Bible that they are true.

▶ **Trust becomes** stronger when you have proven its worth by your actions. Think of times past when God was faithful to you. He promises never to leave you.

▶ **Fear blocks** God's answers, while faith boldly waits for His guidance. Trust Him for His leading and His perfect timing.

> *Understand, therefore, that the LORD your God is indeed God. He is the faithful God who keeps his covenant for a thousand generations and lavishes his unfailing love on those who love him and obey his commands.*
> Deuteronomy 7:9, NLT

What does God promise about living the Christian life?

I will give you a new heart and put a new spirit in you; I will remove from you your heart of stone and give you a heart of flesh. And I will put my Spirit in you and move you to follow my decrees and be careful to keep my laws.

Ezekiel 36:26–27, NIV

question

▼

Does God promise to bless your thoughts?

Concentration is difficult when so many things are vying for focus in your life. You sit down to work on a project, and first thing you know, your mind is off and running, chasing scattered thoughts. You wonder what you should wear to the office get-together or whether you should trade cars, and on it goes. How important are the things you think about? Do they make a difference in your overall life? If they do, what does God want you to think about?

answer

▼

When Moses led the Israelites out of Egypt, they wandered for many years in the wilderness. The main reason was that they let their thoughts control their actions. Since their thoughts were negative, so were their actions. They practiced selective thinking and remembered only parts of the truth. One entire generation missed out on the Promised Land. The same thing can happen to people today. Negative thinking can keep you in the wilderness and cause you to miss God's promised blessings.

Before the Israelites entered the Promised Land, God told them what to think about. It is still applicable to you today. "Love the LORD your God with all your heart, soul, and strength. Memorize his laws and tell them to your children over and over again. Talk about them all the time, whether you're at home or walking along the road or going to bed at night, or getting up in the morning. Write down copies and tie them to your wrists and foreheads to help you obey them. Write these laws on the door frames of your homes and on your town gates" (Deuteronomy 6:5–9, CEV). God wants you to meditate on His laws and principles.

The psalmist tells you that those who think about God's laws are like a tree planted by the water. They do not get tired of working for God. God blesses them with success. When you think about God's law, you gain wisdom and understanding. Your thinking will affect your actions for good.

worth thinking about

▶ **Guard your thoughts** for they are the source of your life. Thoughts are connected. One thought triggers another like itself. Your thoughts will cause you to act in either a positive or a negative manner.

▶ **Fix your thoughts** on Jesus. Focusing on Jesus clears away the distractions of the world. Think on what is really important and what will last.

▶ **Change your way** of thinking. Let God do His work in you. Let your thinking become God thinking.

> *Let the words of my mouth and the meditation of my heart be acceptable to you, O LORD, my rock and my redeemer.*
>
> Psalm 19:14, NRSV

question

What is God's promise when you dismiss grudges and forgive?

When you attempt to put out the flame of bitterness by forgiving, you find that a grudge is still smoldering. You know that you're supposed to forgive others and let go of resentment, but that's easier said than done. Why is it necessary to forgive? After all, sometimes being angry feels justifiable. Maybe you do not want to let it go. How can you forgive and let go of grudges? Will God help you? What are His promises when you do?

answer

"If you become angry, do not let your anger lead you into sin, and do not stay angry all day. Don't give the Devil a chance" (Ephesians 4:26–27, GNT). When you bear a grudge, you give Satan an invitation to fill your mind with his evil and negative thoughts. This festering of evil and negative thoughts produces more of the same, and you begin a downward spiral.

God knows that an unforgiving spirit will steal your peace, so He calls you to forgive and let go of resentment. He promises to help. "Don't try to get even. Trust the LORD, and he will help you" (Proverbs 20:22, CEV).

Forgiveness is a choice. Letting go of a grudge is a choice. You cannot forgive and let go of grudges in your own strength, but you can do it with God's strength.

Jesus taught that you are to forgive others as God has forgiven you. He promised that God would forgive you as you forgive others. Peter, one of Jesus' disciples, asked how often he should forgive someone who had hurt him. Peter suggested seven as a likely number. Imagine Peter's shock when Jesus replied that he should forgive seventy times seven. Forgiving and letting go of grudges may be a process where you make the choice repeatedly until finally, through God's enabling power, you succeed.

worth thinking about

- ▶ **God promises peace**, which gives life to your spirit. He says not to resent or compare your life to another's. Each person must look to Him and choose what is important.

- ▶ **Nursing an unforgiving** spirit—the Scriptures call it a root of bitterness—can actually destroy a life. It eats away at a person's spirit like a disease.

- ▶ **God promises** to help you shut the door to negative thoughts. Give your anger to God, and He will help you forgive.

> *You shall not take vengeance or bear a grudge against any of your people, but you shall love your neighbor as yourself: I am the LORD.*
> Leviticus 19:18, NRSV

question

What are God's promises when you give generously?

Many rich celebrities share their abundance with others. That is admirable, but how can an ordinary person make a difference in the world? Better yet, what does God expect you to do? You've worked hard to get what you have, and it could easily be depleted if you give to every needy cause that asks. How do you choose which ones to support? Does the Bible give any clear direction and promises regarding financial giving?

answer

God issued a challenge to Israel: "I am the LORD All-Powerful, and I challenge you to put me to the test. Bring the entire ten percent into the storehouse, so there will be food in my house. Then I will open the windows of heaven and flood you with blessing after blessing" (Malachi 3:10, CEV). The 10 percent that God refers to is called a tithe. God was asking them to bring 10 percent of their earnings, or harvest, into His storehouse, which was located in the temple. The promise is that you cannot outgive God. He will pour out an abundance of good things on you when you tithe.

When you give to the needy, above the tithe, that is considered an offering. "Watch out! Don't do your good deeds publicly, to be admired by others, for you will lose the reward from your Father in heaven. . . . Give your gifts in private, and your Father, who sees everything, will reward you" (Matthew 6:1, 4, NLT). God is interested in the motives behind your giving. He promises to reward you if you are giving from a generous heart and not from a desire to be applauded for your actions.

Jesus taught that the measure you use will be the measure by which He gives to you. Your measure will be in comparison to your trust in Him. He promises to bless your giving.

worth thinking about

▶ **God is the** Creator of all things. Mankind is the caretaker. God has provided you with everything you have. He blesses you with good things while you are here.

▶ **God loves** a cheerful giver. God wants you to give from a willing heart and not feel pressured into giving. He knows your needs, but He promises to bless your giving.

▶ **Honor God** with your giving. In turn He will bless you.

> *God is able to give you more than you need,*
> *so that you will always have all you need*
> *for yourselves and more than enough*
> *for every good cause.*
> 2 Corinthians 9:8, GNT

question

What are God's promises when you offer hospitality?

Whenever your city hosts a civic event, you are asked to extend the hand of hospitality to visitors. You'll be asked either to entertain in your home or to give up hours at work to show visitors around, hours that you could spend on a project. You do not feel like doing either. It is not that you're antisocial, but you really do value your time and privacy. Does God give promises that support opening your heart and home to others?

answer

God always wants you to be kind. "Remember to welcome strangers in your homes. There were some who did that and welcomed angels without knowing it" (Hebrews 13:2, GNT). Abraham, a great leader of Israel, was one who did entertain angels, and the story is told in Genesis 18. The promise is that good things are in store for those who welcome others.

God understands the restraints on a busy schedule, but He recognizes that making a guest feel welcome is important. Jesus taught that while details are important, making your guest feel welcome is an even greater consideration. God points out in the Scriptures that when you serve others, it is as if you are serving Him. "The king will answer them, 'Truly I tell you, just as you did it to one of the least of these who are members of my family, you did it to me'" (Matthew 25:40, NRSV). He promises to honor your service to others by inviting you to accept your inheritance, which is being a part of His heavenly kingdom.

When you willingly open your home to guests, God often enables the guest to bless you in some way. You may be invited to visit them, or they may be able to connect you with an important contact. God always gives good things to those who do His will.

worth thinking about

- ▶ **Strangers are friends** you haven't met. "Take care of God's needy people and welcome strangers into your home" (Romans 12:13, CEV). Making a new friend is a blessing.

- ▶ **Opportunity is your** chance to be a good representative. "Conduct yourselves wisely toward outsiders, making the most of the time. Let your speech always be gracious, seasoned with salt" (Colossians 4:5–6, NRSV).

- ▶ **God's network** is God at work. God brings good things to your life through other people. "When I come to you, I know that I shall come with a full measure of the blessing of Christ" (Romans 15:29, GNT).

> *Cheerfully share your home with those who need a meal or a place to stay. God has given each of you a gift from his great variety of spiritual gifts. Use them well to serve one another.*
>
> 1 Peter 4:9–10, NLT

80

question
▼
How does God promise to protect you?

Big city or small town, danger seems to lurk around every corner. The media make sure you know of all possible encounters. If you dwelled on all the frightening possibilities, you'd be afraid to leave your home. Still, you have to live, and the sensible part of you says that staying in is not a choice. After all, harm can come knocking on the door of your house. How does God promise to protect you?

answer
▼

One way that God offers you protection is for you to call out His name. The mere utterance of His name brings angels to surround you. "The name of the LORD is a strong fortress; the godly run to him and are safe" (Proverbs 18:10, NLT). God promises to protect you by His name.

The psalmist said that God inhabits praise. When you praise God for who He is—your Creator, your Hope, your Savior, the list is endless—His presence surrounds you. When the presence of God surrounds you, His protection abounds. One sure way to send the enemy running is to start praising God. The armies of biblical times learned that going into battle praising God would bring victory. Praise not only brings protection from physical dangers, but it also protects you mentally and spiritually. Praise will protect you from depressing or negative thoughts.

Prayer puts you in the presence of God. Jesus said, "Where two or three are gathered in my name, I am there among them" (Matthew 18:20, NRSV). Being in the presence of God is like having a protective shield surround you.

God also protects by providing you with His spiritual armor. Ephesians 6:10–18 explains the meaning of each piece of armor. It recommends that you put on the knowledge of your salvation as a helmet. Then wear His goodness as a breastplate and His truth as a belt. Place His shoes of peace on your feet. Use your faith in Him as a shield, and carry His Word as a sword. Always remember to pray.

worth thinking about

▶ **God is a shield.** He shields you with His promises as you believe them. He encompasses you with protection and surrounds you with angels.

▶ **God is a refuge.** When you are feeling down and out, you can seek His presence in prayer, and He promises peace. You will feel safe in His love.

▶ **God is a deliverer.** Psalm 91 says God will be with you in trouble and rescue you from danger. He even promises that His angels will lift you out of harm's way.

> *Find rest, O my soul, in God alone; my hope comes from him. He alone is my rock and my salvation; he is my fortress, I will not be shaken.*
> Psalm 62:5–6, NIV

81

question

Does God promise to help you change?

Developing new and better habits is difficult, but it is something you desire. Research says that if you stick with a new action for three weeks, it becomes a habit. That sounds good, but you're not sure how real change evolves. You ran into an old friend the other day who is doing well. When you commented on the positive changes in his life, he accredited them to God. Can God really help you change for the better?

answer

When you seek God and choose Him as Lord of your life, He will help you get rid of bad habits and make positive changes. He sends His Holy Spirit to live within you. "Humans give life to their children. Yet only God's Spirit can change you into a child of God. . . . Only God's Spirit gives new life" (John 3:6, 8, CEV).

When you choose to leave old habits behind, God's Spirit will help you form new ones. That is His promise to you. Over time, you will discover that you have been transformed by His power working inside you. "Everything—and I do mean everything—connected with that old way of life has to go. It's rotten through and through. Get rid of it! And then take on an entirely new way of life—a God-fashioned life, a life renewed from the inside and working itself into your conduct as God accurately reproduces his character in you" (Ephesians 4:22–24, THE MESSAGE).

Change is a process. But as you read the Bible, spend time with His followers, and begin talking to God in prayer, you will find that you are getting stronger in your inner being.

Paul warned the new followers in Rome not to conform to the world's standards. He encouraged them to let God change the way they thought so that they would choose to live differently. God would transform all their bad habits into positive new ones that would honor Him. God promises that your new life will emerge and that you will be filled with His love and kindness.

worth thinking about

▶ **God promises** to transform your heart. God promises to give you a new spiritual heart, one that comes from His Holy Spirit living in you.

▶ **God promises** to renew you with His love. Gradually, you will come to realize the depth of His love. Then you will let His love motivate your actions.

▶ **God promises** to reshape your life. God will change you completely, inside and out. Thinking God's thoughts will define your life with a new pattern of activity.

> *What I say is this: let the Spirit direct your lives, and you will not satisfy the desires of the human nature.*
>
> Galatians 5:16, GNT

question

What does God promise when you control your tongue?

Talking without thinking is a dangerous way of life. The tongue can be a mighty weapon to offend people, make them angry, or harm their reputations. How do you handle damage control—pretend it didn't happen, or apologize? The consequences of a loose tongue can mar relationships for years. There have been many times you've wished you'd kept better control of your words. Will God help you? Does He make any promises about controlling your tongue?

answer

James the Apostle likened the tongue to a spark that can start a forest fire. He went on to say that while many wild animals can be tamed, the tongue is hard to control. The only way to do it is to seek God's help. The psalmist prayed, "Set a guard over my mouth, O LORD; keep watch over the door of my lips" (Psalm 141:3, NIV). God will help you just as He helped the psalmist; you only have to ask.

God gives many promises regarding the benefits of learning to control your speech. The psalmist said if you want to live and enjoy a long life, then you have to stop lying and saying cruel things. Fighting and fussing will raise your blood pressure. Telling lies will fill you with anxiety, and a life of deception may even endanger your life. God's plan for you is to enjoy peace and live a long and healthy life.

"Watch your words and hold your tongue; you'll save yourself a lot of grief" (Proverbs 21:23, THE MESSAGE). This wise proverb offers godly advice about controlling your speech. God promises that if you seek His help and think before speaking, you won't have to suffer the feelings of regret or the turmoil your words may cause. Your health and physical safety will benefit from this, and you will have long life.

worth thinking about

▶ **Change your heart;** change your words. The Bible tells you to let God's commandments live in you. When you know God's promises, they will make you wise in the way you act.

▶ **Ask God** to help you control your tongue. James wrote that you need to learn to be a good listener and then to learn to think before you speak. You must learn to control your anger and not fly off the handle at every little thing. Snapping at people won't bring God's peace.

▶ **God promises** that you can represent Him when you allow Him to teach you and help you control your tongue. Then you will speak words that uplift, which always produce God's peace.

> We pray that our Lord Jesus Christ and God our Father will encourage you and help you always to do and say the right thing.
> 2 Thessalonians 2:16–17, CEV

question

Does God promise to help you control your anger?

You've been told you have a short fuse, and it is true. Your anger spews out quickly, and then it is over—that's how you've justified it. It cannot be that bad if you get over it immediately. But lately you've realized you have a problem. You find yourself snapping at everyone. You often blurt out things that would be better left unsaid. Can God help you control your anger? Is there a secret or a solution to controlling your temper?

answer

Paul, a worker for God, wrote, "Be angry but do not sin; do not let the sun go down on your anger" (Ephesians 4:26, NRSV). Anger is an emotion that God created within you. Although the anger may be a natural reaction, you need to release it in a constructive way. Choose to give your anger to God emotionally. Release the physical energy that anger produces through some healthy exercise. Your anger will bring terrible consequences if you lash out verbally or harm someone physically. God knows that anger needs to be dealt with immediately, or else it will poison your thinking.

The Bible includes much wisdom about anger control. "A kind answer soothes angry feelings, but harsh words stir them up" (Proverbs 15:1, CEV). Anger sparks anger, while a gentle answer makes people want to cooperate.

Paul wrote to the Galatians, "When you follow the desires of your sinful nature, the results are very clear: . . . hostility, quarreling, jealousy, outbursts of anger, selfish ambition, dissension, division, and other sins like these" (Galatians 5:19–20, NLT).

He encouraged them, and it is applicable to you today, to seek God's Spirit for help. God can and will help you control your quick temper if you rely on His Spirit for guidance.

worth thinking about

▶ **Anger can be** a habit. Learn a new habit. Form your reply with the exact words and tone you would want someone to use when speaking to you.

▶ **Squelch your angry** replies by speaking to honor God. Keep in mind that He hears everything you say and that a kind answer pleases Him.

▶ **Give your anger** to God. "Vengeance is mine, and I won't overlook a thing" (Hebrews 10:30, THE MESSAGE).

> *Put away from you all bitterness and wrath and anger and wrangling and slander, together with all malice, and be kind to one another, tenderhearted, forgiving one another, as God in Christ has forgiven you.*
>
> Ephesians 4:31–32, NRSV

question

Does God promise to help you learn patience?

Patience is not one of your virtues. You admire people who endure hardships and patiently wait for things to smooth out or for answers to come. You wonder how they do it, for you have trouble waiting even in the checkout line. You cannot imagine surviving a long illness or something equally serious. How do people acquire patience? Is it something they are born with, or do they develop patience in the circumstance? What does God have to say about patience?

answer

When you cannot stand the impatient way you act, you realize how badly you need to develop patience. You turn to God and ask Him to do the impossible. God will place His forbearance within you through His Spirit. You seek and allow God's patience to become your patience.

Patience is part of the good that results from troubles and trials. "We know how troubles can develop passionate patience in us, and how that patience in turn forges the tempered steel of virtue, keeping us alert for whatever God will do next" (Romans 5:3–4, THE MESSAGE). Tragedies have a unique way of bringing the important things in life into focus.

It is true that patience grows by leaps and bounds in troubling circumstances, but God also equips you with patience for small matters. "Look for the best in each other, and always do your best to bring it out" (1 Thessalonians 5:15, THE MESSAGE).

Physical muscles develop with exercise, and spiritual development is acquired the same way. Begin to practice godly patience while waiting at the stoplight, while waiting in line, and while caring for others. Acting with patience will soon become a God-given promise in your life.

worth thinking about

▶ **Remind yourself** of God's might. Learning patience is not easy, but God is powerful. "This is the same mighty power that raised Christ from the dead" (Ephesians 1:19–20, NLT).

▶ **Practice patience** daily. Whenever demands are made upon you, think of Jesus surrounded by crowds who were seeking His healing.

▶ **Make a mental** list of the good things in your life. Express thankfulness for each blessing in your life.

> *Do not throw away this confident trust in the Lord. Remember the great reward it brings you! Patient endurance is what you need now, so that you will continue to do God's will. Then you will receive all that he has promised.*
>
> Hebrews 10:35–36, NLT

question

Does God promise to give you victory over temptations?

Temptations seem to offer you happiness until you partake of them, and then their ugly deception is revealed. What once had appealed to you is now revealed as a lie. Sometimes temptations are easily recognized, but generally they sneak up on you and trip you up when you least expect it. It is only after you've fallen that you realize you've been had and that there are consequences to pay. Can God help you recognize temptation before you fall? Does He promise to give you victory over temptation?

answer

God is wisdom, and when you choose to lean on Him, He will give you His wisdom. Knowing God, knowing who He is, and knowing how He has worked in the past provides valuable insight into recognizing temptations. The Bible says, "Don't believe everything you hear. Carefully weigh and examine what people tell you. Not everyone who talks about God comes from God. There are a lot of lying preachers loose in the world. Here's how you test for the genuine Spirit of God. Everyone who confesses openly his faith in Jesus Christ—the Son of God, who came as an actual flesh-and-blood person— comes from God and belongs to God" (1 John 4:1–2,

THE MESSAGE). God will help you discern temptation, but you need to seek His guidance and apply it.

If you are in a tempting situation and do not feel strong enough to get out, God will help you. "The temptations in your life are no different from what others experience. And God is faithful....When you are tempted, he will show you a way out so that you can endure" (1 Corinthians 10:13, NLT). The promise for victory over temptation is twofold. First, He won't let you be tempted above what you can handle, and second, He's providing a way out.

worth thinking about

▶ Do not tempt temptation—run from it. Do not give temptation an opportunity to attack; remove yourself from its grasp, and then God will give you victory.

▶ Remember that temptation does not come from God, but from evil. God is without fault and tempts no one. He is the One who will help you win by beating out temptation.

▶ Enduring temptations and allowing God to help you escape will strengthen your trust in Him. You will know that what God says, He will do.

> *To him who is able to keep you from falling and to present you before his glorious presence without fault and with great joy—to the only God our Savior be glory, majesty, power and authority, through Jesus Christ our Lord.*
> Jude 1:24–25, NIV

question

What does God promise about shaping your character?

answer

He who began a good work in you will carry it on to completion until the day of Christ Jesus.

Philippians 1:6, NIV

86 question

Does God promise to produce His character traits in you?

Lately, you've been taking stock of your life: how you've changed, and how you'd like to change. If only you could smooth out the rough edges of your personality and be kinder and more caring toward people. Looking back, you can see the point where you started pulling away from God and chose to go your own way. If you start drawing close to Him now, will He promise to put His character traits within you?

answer

When you go to God and align your life with His, you choose to take on His nature. You get rid of your old style of living. "Chosen by God for this new life of love, dress in the wardrobe God picked out for you: compassion, kindness, humility, quiet strength, discipline. Be even-tempered, content with second place, quick to forgive an offense. Forgive as quickly and completely as the Master forgave you. And regardless of what else you put on, wear love. It's your basic, all-purpose garment. Never be without it" (Colossians 3:12–14, The Message).

You choose God's character traits, and He makes them available to you by His Holy Spirit within you. The Scriptures teach that love, joy peace, patience, kindness, goodness, faithfulness, gentleness, and self-control are all products, or fruit, of God's Spirit. When you turn to God, He will produce His traits in your life.

The message of Paul's letter to the people of Philippi is still applicable today: "I am certain that God, who began the good work within you, will continue his work until it is finally finished on that day when Christ Jesus returns" (Philippians 1:6, NLT). When you start to grow in God, there is a struggle with your old nature and your new nature. God will be producing and growing His characteristics in you during your entire life. He never gives up on you.

worth thinking about

▶ **God's promise** to produce His characteristics in your life is contingent upon you. When someone gives you a gift, you make the choice of whether you will accept or not accept it. If you accept the gift, what you do with it is up to you.

▶ **Plants draw** nutrients from their roots. You must draw your spiritual nutrients from God. He will produce His fruit in you.

▶ **Be patient** as God produces His character in you. "Do not be weary in doing what is right" (2 Thessalonians 3:13, NRSV). God is faithful to His promise.

May you always be filled with the fruit of your salvation—the righteous character produced in your life by Jesus Christ—for this will bring much glory and praise to God.

Philippians 1:11, NLT

87

question
▼
What is God's promise for meeting with other believers?

Life is extremely busy in this day and age, yet a great deal of importance is placed on church attendance. What is to be gained by giving up half a day to meet with other churchgoers? Wouldn't it be just as effective to have a time of daily meditation? Sunday is supposed to be a day of rest. What is God's reasoning when He asks you to meet with His followers? Does He make a promise about meeting with other believers?

answer
▼

When people first commit their lives to God, they may not understand how they will benefit by attending church regularly. God in His wisdom knows that His followers need one another. "We should keep on encouraging each other to be thoughtful and to do helpful things. Some people have gotten out of the habit of meeting for worship, but we must not do that. We should keep on encouraging each other" (Hebrews 10:24–25, CEV). The reason and the promise are the same: if you meet with God's followers, He promises that you'll be encouraged and that you will encourage others.

When you are in a group of God's followers, if you have a problem, someone will help you. If they are struggling, you will be there to help them. "Two are better off than one, because together they can work more effectively. If one of them falls down, the other can help him up. But if someone is alone and falls, it's just too bad, because there is no one to help him" (Ecclesiastes 4:9–10, GNT). Again, you see the promise of encouragement.

God gives all His followers talents and abilities. "The Spirit's presence is shown in some way in each person for the good of all" (1 Corinthians 12:7, GNT). When they unite and start working together, it is like they become the body of Jesus—for the body has many parts, and each one has a different purpose. God's promise is evident; people serve and encourage one another.

worth thinking about

- ▶ **You will have** a support system. The group of God's people that you meet with will be a strong framework of support when you face difficulties. They will assist you with everyday details that you cannot do for yourself.

- ▶ **When your faith** is weak, others who follow God can help your faith flame brightly by sharing lessons from Scripture and from their own lives.

- ▶ **In turn,** when others need your assistance, you will grow by giving of yourself and ministering to them. All are strengthened and encouraged by meeting together.

> *I pray that the LORD will listen when you are in trouble, and that the God of Jacob will keep you safe. May the LORD send help from his temple and come to your rescue from Mount Zion.*
>
> Psalm 20:1–2, CEV

question

What does God's promise to set you free really mean?

Everyone understands the concept of prison, but many people live in self-imposed prisons. They have let relationships, damaged emotions, addictions, and similar situations lock them up. They want to be free and pretend to be free, but when they try to move forward, they hit a wall. Does God promise to set you free from these types of self-imprisonments when you come to Him? What does it mean when God promises to set you free?

answer

During the time of the Old Testament, people lived under the laws handed down from God to Moses. When their acts and attitudes displeased God, they found forgiveness by offering the required sacrifices. They were always struggling with guilt, though, because it was impossible to live a perfect life and keep every law.

When Jesus came, He brought freedom from the law by giving the gift of grace. Grace is receiving that which you do not deserve. No one is deserving of grace because "all have sinned and fall short of the glory of God, and are justified freely by his grace through the redemption that came by Christ Jesus" (Romans 3:23–24, NIV).

God longs to free you from guilt. It is not His plan for you to be imprisoned by damaged emotions or addictions. He made a way for you to live worry-free. He offers you grace through His Son. You are freed from condemnation when you choose to accept Jesus. "Christ was sacrificed once to take away the sins of many people" (Hebrews 9:28, NIV). Not only is your guilt absolved, but you have freedom from your anxieties and bad habits. You do not have to let those negatives tie up your life. This does not mean you won't have to do your part. You choose to let God work in your life. You choose to place your trust in Him, believing that He will do what He says, but He frees you and will teach you.

worth thinking about

▶ **Your beliefs** affect the way you act. Believe God's promise—you are free in Jesus, which means you can lay down that backpack of problems.

▶ **Say good-bye** to regrets over past mistakes. He gives you grace instead of guilt. When accusing thoughts nag at you, remind yourself that you are now living under God's grace.

▶ **Listen to God's** truth as written in the Scriptures, as spoken to you by others, and as His Spirit whispers to you in prayer. Do not listen to the voice of your damaged emotions. You are freed to think a new way.

> *I am telling you the truth: everyone who sins is a slave of sin. A slave does not belong to a family permanently, but a son belongs there forever. If the Son sets you free, then you will be really free.*
>
> John 8:34–36, GNT

question

Does God promise to give you an identity in Him?

People search to discover their individual identity, what they believe in and what provides them with a sense of belonging. Many pursue the quest their entire lives, trying on one set of beliefs after another, supporting different causes, or changing careers frequently. Nothing feels right. They long to discover something or someone who will give life meaning. Is the search a spiritual one? Does God promise to give meaning to your life and an identity in Him?

answer

When you choose to follow Jesus and accept His forgiveness, you are adopted into the family of God. Your spiritual decision identifies you as a member of God's family and as His child. You are now a joint heir with Jesus.

The Bible is filled with promises for how God shapes your identity in Him. He has a special plan for your life. "We are what he has made us, created in Christ Jesus for good works, which God prepared beforehand to be our way of life" (Ephesians 2:10, NRSV). God equips you with the things you need to serve. He gave you just the right talents and abilities to do those good works He planned. Now He will call them into action. God will give you satisfaction and joy in your work, which will make daily life a pleasure.

God will go with you through trials and troubles. He will strengthen and teach you as you spend your life learning about Him. He will guide you in your decisions and give good things to you. Your new identity in Him does not end with this world. Because of your relationship with Him, you will spend eternity with Him. All of these promises are from God and are an assurance that He will give you a new identity.

worth thinking about

▶ God marks your new identity in Him by His love. He fills you up with it. The Bible says that people will know you are His follower by your love.

▶ God makes you His representative when you choose to find your identity in Him. You are His light in the world. You influence those in the world instead of letting them influence you.

▶ Another identity marker will be your faith in God. Others will see that you are trusting in Him for your strength, your daily provisions, and for all things.

> *Anyone who belongs to Christ is a new person.*
> *The past is forgotten, and everything is new.*
> 2 Corinthians 5:17, CEV

question

Does God promise to give you faith?

Believing in something that cannot be seen or that you do not fully understand is difficult. Still, a certain amount of trust is required every day of your life. You get in your car and travel to work, although you may not fully comprehend how the engine works. A flip of a switch produces electricity, even if you do not understand electrical wiring. But your concern is with a deeper subject. Does God promise to give you faith to believe in Him?

answer

God is invisible to mankind. But the faith He places in hearts gives the assurance that He is real. The Scriptures teach that you are saved by faith in Him, and that God Himself gives it as a gift. You have to choose what to do with His gift of faith. If you do not take a stand and make the choice to believe, you will constantly be tossed to and fro—sometimes believing, sometimes doubting. "If you are like that, unable to make up your mind and undecided in all you do, you must not think that you will receive anything from the Lord" (James 1:7–8, GNT).

Just as physical muscles atrophy if not used, the spiritual muscle of faith will do the same. It has to be exercised.

"Without faith it is impossible to please God, because anyone who comes to him must believe that he exists and that he rewards those who earnestly seek him" (Hebrews 11:6, NIV). Your trust in Him tells God that you believe He is there. God will give you plenty of opportunities to exercise your faith. Each time you rely on your faith to get you through a trial, God will reward you. Your faith will keep expanding until it will be strong enough to carry you through any circumstance. Your faith will be an encouragement to others, for they will see that God does indeed promise the gift of faith.

worth thinking about

▶ A gift that can be used over and over is the best one to receive. An heirloom increases in value. A faith that is active just keeps getting better and better.

▶ Choosing to believe produces peace, while entertaining doubts causes stress and additionally blocks answers.

▶ Trials are opportunities to exercise your gift of faith. "The testing of your faith produces endurance; and let endurance have its full effect, so that you may be mature and complete, lacking in nothing" (James 1:3–4, NRSV).

> Whatever is born of God conquers the world. And this is the victory that conquers the world, our faith.
>
> 1 John 5:4, NRSV

91

question

Does God use angels to carry out His promises?

Angels have intrigued people since the beginning of time. Some people collect replicas of angels. One glance at a collection of angels, and it is plain to see that people perceive angels differently. There is also confusion over how angels came to be. Some people even suggest that people become angels when they die. What is God's truth regarding angels? Do they have special roles? Do they help carry out His promises to mankind?

answer

Angels are created beings. "God created everything in heaven and on earth, the seen and the unseen" (Colossians 1:16, GNT). People do not die and become angels. People and angels are both created beings of God and have different purposes.

The Old and New Testaments tell of incidents when angels were actually sighted. The Bible says that angels can take on human forms, and that you may be unaware of their presence. People are encouraged to extend a warm welcome to their homes, for the Bible states that some people have entertained angels unaware.

God created angels to minister to and protect His people. "Angels are only servants—spirits sent to care for people who will inherit salvation" (Hebrews 1:14, NLT). An angel ministered to Elijah by providing food and water when he was in need. Angels have served as messengers on numerous occasions. They were the ones sent by God to proclaim the birth of Jesus to the shepherds. They also demonstrate might and power. The angels rolled the stone away from Jesus' tomb. They serve as protectors. God sent an angel to shut the mouth of the lions when King Darius threw Daniel in the lions' den. God uses His angels to carry out promises to His followers.

worth thinking about

▶ **Whether seen** or unseen, angels surround you. Believe that God is carrying out His promises to shield and protect you. The Bible says, "The angel of the LORD encamps around those who fear him, and he delivers them" (Psalm 34:7, NIV).

▶ **God's angels** still minister today. They encourage you by sending someone to help at your precise moment of need, or by intervening on your behalf themselves.

▶ **God's angels** provide supernatural strength in emergency situations. There are many stories about people who were enabled to do heroic acts of rescue. Based on the testimony of the Scriptures, God's angels may be assisting them.

> *He will command his angels concerning you to guard you in all your ways. On their hands they will bear you up, so that you will not dash your foot against a stone.*
> Psalm 91:11–12, NRSV

question

▼

Does God promise you can know you're going to heaven?

People do not like to think about death. They try to avoid thinking about it unless the subject is forced upon them by an illness. Most people like to think that death is something way out in the future. But time passes, and the moment arrives when they must face the fact that death is a part of living. Whatever the reason, there comes a moment when everyone must give thought to where they will spend eternity. Does God promise that you can really know your eternal destination?

answer

▼

Jesus taught, "I am the way and the truth and the life. No one comes to the Father except through me" (John 14:6, NIV). The way, the truth, and the life He is talking about is the fact that you are no longer condemned when you accept that He died for you. Believing and aligning your life with God gives life. The promise of life with God applies both to life here on earth and then in heaven. "By grace you have been saved through faith, and this is not your own doing; it is the gift of God—not the result of works, so that no one may boast" (Ephesians 2:8–9, NRSV). It is not possible to save yourself. You cannot earn your way to heaven by doing good works, although it is true that you will be rewarded for those works.

Jesus was the Good Shepherd, and He often referred to His followers as His sheep. "My sheep know my voice, and I know them. They follow me, and I give them eternal life, so that they will never be lost. No one can snatch them out of my hand" (John 10:27–28, CEV). God's Spirit lives within you, but when you leave this earth, you will go to heaven to spend eternity with the triune God (Father, Son, and Holy Spirit). The promise is that you can know that heaven is your eternal destination.

worth thinking about

▶ You will always be with God. He has given His gift and promise. Your life is wrapped up in His.

▶ God's promise of eternal life in heaven fills you with love. You do not have to work for Him, but because of His gift, you cannot do enough. You want to share His good news with others, too.

▶ God's Spirit within you is like a guarantee of your heavenly life with Him. It is an inheritance within you, an assurance of more to come.

> *God loved the world so much that he gave his one and only Son, so that everyone who believes in him will not perish but have eternal life.*
> John 3:16, NLT

93

question

What promise was given about Jesus' return?

There is much documentation in Matthew, Mark, Luke, and John that Jesus truly did come to earth as an infant, lived to be a man, died a cruel death, and arose after three days in the tomb. It was reported later that He returned to heaven. Some people say that He will return to earth someday, and you'd like to learn more about it. What was the exact promise He made before returning to heaven?

answer

Before Jesus' death, He had a heart-to-heart talk with His disciples. He wanted to prepare them for His death, resurrection, and return to heaven. "Don't let this throw you. You trust God, don't you? Trust me. There is plenty of room for you in my Father's home. If that weren't so, would I have told you that I'm on my way to get a room ready for you? And if I'm on my way to get your room ready, I'll come back and get you so you can live where I live" (John 14:1–3, THE MESSAGE). Nothing as astounding as this had ever happened before. They didn't fully understand the promise. Later, it would become clearer.

Jesus added, "It is better for you that I go away, because if I do not go, the Helper will not come to you. But if I do go away, then I will send him to you" (John 16:7, GNT). Jesus would send the Holy Spirit to live within them. Jesus warned that His return would be as quick as lightning, and they needed to be prepared. No one except the Father would know the exact date. Jesus had given the promise, and in the Book of Acts the first part is fulfilled.

Jesus ascended right in front of the disciples, hidden by a cloud. The fulfillment of the second half of the promise still waits.

worth thinking about

- ▶ **Matthew 24** tells about the days before Jesus' promised return. Certain signs will indicate His return is near.

- ▶ **Jesus told** the thief on the cross that he would be with Him in Paradise that day. When God's followers die, their spirits go to heaven immediately, but their earthly bodies are buried. The Bible teaches that there will be a bodily resurrection with Jesus' promised return.

- ▶ **Live in expectation** of His promised return. "With the Lord one day is like a thousand years, and a thousand years are like one day" (2 Peter 3:8, NRSV).

Why do you stand here looking into the sky? This same Jesus, who has been taken from you into heaven, will come back in the same way you have seen him go into heaven.

Acts 1:11, NIV

question

Does God promise eternal rewards?

Eternal life in heaven is given when you make Jesus the Lord of your life. It is a gift of grace, and it cannot be earned through good works. Your understanding of this is clear, until you hear someone speak of earning eternal rewards. Then you're confused. What are eternal awards? If life in heaven is a gift of grace, how do you earn rewards? Does God promise eternal rewards?

answer

The teachings of Jesus indicate that there are heavenly rewards; His promises are evident. In Matthew 6, Jesus said not to worry about getting rich on earth but to do things that will please God and earn riches in heaven. The promise is evident. Since eternal life with God is a gift of grace, heavenly riches would be additional rewards.

Jesus warns that correct motives are important. God rewards sincere motives. He cautions His followers not to do good deeds to impress others, nor to make a big show of using fancy words when they pray.

Although the writers of the Bible did not explain exactly what the heavenly rewards will be, the promises are there. Crowns, given as rewards, are referred to throughout the Scriptures. Paul wrote about receiving a crown of righteousness, and then he spoke of a crown that will last forever. Other biblical writers mentioned crowns, too. Peter and James mentioned receiving the crown of glory, and James referred to the crown of life.

In 1 Corinthians 3:11–15, Paul likens the believer's life to building a house. The foundation is Jesus. The things you do are the building materials. Your building blocks will be tested at Jesus' return, and if they last, you will earn the promised heavenly rewards. If they do not, you will still enter heaven by grace if you are a child of God.

worth thinking about

- ▶ Let love be behind your question, What can I do for Jesus? When you work from that premise, you do not have to question why you are serving.

- ▶ God knows that if you're willing to give without recognition or serve without applause, your motives are sincere.

- ▶ Give to those who cannot repay you. "You will be blessed. Although they cannot repay you, you will be repaid at the resurrection of the righteous" (Luke 14:14, NIV).

> Let us not become weary in doing good, for at the proper time we will reap a harvest if we do not give up. Therefore, as we have opportunity, let us do good to all people, especially to those who belong to the family of believers.
>
> Galatians 6:9–10, NIV

95 question

What does God promise heaven will be like?

Heaven must be a wonderful place. Everything you've ever read or heard indicates that truth. You've always been told that it will be a filled with happiness. How wonderful! But when it comes to actually picturing heaven, you envision an ultramodern space station. Where did that image come from? Are you just trying to imagine something completely different from the world? What does the Bible teach about heaven? Does God give any promises about heaven?

answer

When Jesus returns to earth and the judgment is passed, a new heaven and earth will appear. "The first heaven and the first earth disappeared, and the sea vanished. And I saw the Holy City, the New Jerusalem, coming down out of heaven from God" (Revelation 21:1–2, GNT). God will live with His people in this new heaven and earth. God will wipe away all tears, for there won't be any sorrow or pain.

The New Jerusalem won't need the sun or moon, and there won't be any night. "The glory of God made the city bright. It was dazzling and crystal clear like a precious jasper stone" (Revelation 21:11, CEV). The city will be a perfect cube with high, thick walls, set upon twelve foundation stones made of precious gems. The names of the twelve apostles will be inscribed upon the stones.

Each wall of the city will have three pearl gates guarded by angels. The names of the twelve tribes of Israel will be inscribed on the gates, and the gates will never close. The main street will be paved with transparent gold. There won't be a temple; there will be only the throne of God and His Son, Jesus. A river of life will flow from the throne, down the main street. Trees that produce a different fruit each month will grow on each side of the river.

worth thinking about

- ▶ Picture the earth without weeds or blemishes. The description of the new heaven and the new earth shows that God will keep His promise to restore nature.

- ▶ God's new heaven and new earth include the promise that He will dwell with His people. All who accept the gift of grace are citizens of heaven.

- ▶ Time and measurement, as you know them, are part of God's promise. Twelve months are mentioned. "He measured the city with his rod, fifteen hundred miles; its length and width and height are equal" (Revelation 21:16, NRSV).

> I looked again. I saw a huge crowd, too huge to count. Everyone was there—all nations and tribes, all races and languages. And they were standing, dressed in white robes and waving palm branches, standing before the Throne and the Lamb and heartily singing.
>
> Revelation 7:9–10, THE MESSAGE

What does God promise about eternity?

I know whom I have believed, and am convinced that he is able to guard what I have entrusted to him for that day.

2 Timothy 1:12, NIV

question

▼

What are God's promises concerning death?

The most frightening thing about death is the unknown. People do not want to give up the known for the unknown. They love their family and friends and choose to stay with them. Most people cling to this life so tightly that they refuse to make a will until the latter part of life. But are there things you can know about death that would soothe or ease your fears? What do the Scriptures teach about dying? Does God give any promises regarding death?

answer

▼

The Bible teaches that there is life after death. Everyone will spend eternity in one of two places: in heaven or hell. But there are many wonderful promises relating to death for those who have chosen Jesus as their Lord. Physical death won't separate God from His followers; it will unite them. Believers will get to see God's face.

God's promises will ease the transition from physical death to eternal life in heaven. Depending on a person's physical condition, death may even be a welcome release. Physical death resulted from the unconditional covenant being broken in the Garden of Eden. But thanks to Jesus, you can have the gift of eternal life in heaven.

God promises that heaven is going to be spectacular—
that you cannot even imagine how wonderful it is going
to be. Jesus promised that He was preparing a special
place for each person.

When Jesus was dying on the cross, He was placed
between two thieves. One of the thieves was really repen-
tant and was sorry for what he had done. Jesus forgave
him. When you die, your spirit goes immediately to be
with Jesus. Your earthly body is left behind. Paul stated
that to be absent from your earthly body is to be present
with God. He explained that in heaven you will have a
new and different kind of body.

worth thinking about

▶ **Psalm 23:4 promises** that God will walk you
through the valley of the shadow of death. He has
already promised never to leave you.

▶ **God promises** that death has lost its power. It
can no longer destroy those who call Jesus Lord
(1 Corinthians 15:55–57).

▶ **God promises** that the benefits of heaven—all the
wonderful things He has planned for you—will outweigh any suffering you have experienced on earth.

> *Now all we can see of God is like a cloudy pic-*
> *ture in a mirror. Later we will see him face to*
> *face. We don't know everything, but then we*
> *will, just as God completely understands us.*
>
> 1 Corinthians 13:12, CEV

Does God promise you will recognize loved ones in heaven?

Death separates loved ones. People extend comfort by saying that the person has just gone on—meaning to eternal life—and that you will join him later. You realize that dying is a part of life, and you hope to one day be reunited with your loved one in heaven. Do you want to know what the Bible has to say about this? Are people just assuming you will recognize your loved ones? Does God really make such a promise?

answer
▼

There is nothing specific in the Bible where God says, "Yes, you will know your loved ones in heaven." But there are scriptures that imply you will. Paul wrote in 1 Thessalonians 4 that he did not want you to grieve over loved ones the way people grieve who have no hope. "We believe that Jesus died and was raised to life. We also believe that when God brings Jesus back again, he will bring with him all who had faith in Jesus before they died" (1 Thessalonians 4:14, CEV). This passage seems to imply you will recognize your loved ones, otherwise you would continue to be sad.

Paul also wrote to the Thessalonians, a group of people they had told about Jesus, "What gives us hope and joy, and what will be our proud reward and crown as we stand before our Lord Jesus when he returns? It is you!" (1 Thessalonians 2:19, NLT). Paul was implying both recognition and the grouping together of those he had known on earth.

The Bible promises that those who have faithfully worked for the Lord during their lifetimes will receive rewards in heaven. In order for those rewards to be appreciated, you would have to still be you. Revelation 21 mentions that on the twelve gates to the New Jerusalem, the names of the twelve tribes of Israel are inscribed, and the names of the twelve apostles are written on the foundation stones. If people in heaven do not retain their memories, there wouldn't be any purpose to the inscriptions.

worth thinking about

▶ **Romans 14:12 states** that each person will give a personal account of his life before God. You will still be you in heaven.

▶ **Mary and the** disciples recognized Jesus in His resurrected body (John 20:16; 21:12). Surely you will be recognizable in your resurrected body.

▶ **Relationships will be** different in heaven. But people will still be who they were on earth. In Matthew 8:11, Jesus indicated that you will recognize Abraham, Isaac, and Jacob, who lived in early biblical times.

> *Dear friends, now we are children of God, and what we will be has not yet been made known. But we know that when he appears, we shall be like him, for we shall see him as he is.*
>
> 1 John 3:2, NIV

98

question

Do God's promises reveal heaven's location?

Most people believe in heaven, but they are divided in their opinions of where it is located. Some people believe heaven is here and now, that it is happening within them. Others believe it is up, way beyond the sky and outer space. Then there are those who believe heaven is located in another dimension, one veiled from human eyesight. What does the Bible say about heaven's location? Is it possible to know for sure where heaven is located? Does it really matter?

answer

Heaven is where God abides. When a person chooses God, He takes up residency in the heart. Thus, the concept of heaven within a person is born. Because of this, heaven will be experienced while on earth, but it is only a taste of what will be encountered when one's earthly life ends.

Numerous scriptures state or imply that heaven is located on a higher plane. Jesus ascended into heaven (Luke 24:51). The New Jerusalem will descend from heaven (Revelation 21:2). God took the prophet Elijah up into heaven in a whirlwind (2 Kings 2:11–12), and the psalmist made reference to heaven's being upward.

Humankind refers to both the sky and the universe as the heavens. Since heaven, the place where God lives, is understood to be up and beyond that, it is referred to as the third heaven. Paul wrote, "I know a person in Christ who fourteen years ago was caught up to the third heaven —whether in the body or out of the body I do not know; God knows" (2 Corinthians 12:2, NRSV).

It is true that heaven may be located in the highest realms beyond the universe, and it is definitely true that heaven is not visible to the human eye. But it isn't necessary to pinpoint heaven's exact location for you to joyfully anticipate living there.

worth thinking about

- ▶ **God's plan has** always been to live with those He created. This was impossible after disobedience entered the world, for God cannot live with wrongdoing.

- ▶ **God's love found** a way to bring you into His presence by extending grace (undeserved favor) through His Son. The Bible says all have done wrong and are unworthy (Romans 3:9–12).

- ▶ **After the return** of Jesus and the judgment, a new heaven and a new earth will replace the current heaven and earth. The New Jerusalem will descend from the new heaven to the new earth (Revelation 21:1–2).

> *I heard a loud voice speaking from the throne: "Now God's home is with people! He will live with them, and they shall be his people. God himself will be with them, and he will be their God."*
>
> Revelation 21:3, GNT

99

question
▾

Does God promise what your heavenly body will be like?

People are not only curious about heaven, but they are also curious about the bodies they will have. Some people argue that people will just be spirits, while others believe they will become like angels. Still others speculate that heavenly bodies will possess supernatural powers and be able to go through walls, maybe even dematerialize and materialize in another place. You suppose anything is possible. Does God promise what type of bodies people will possess?

answer
▾

Jesus died a physical death and rose again in His resurrected body. Scriptures reveal that His friends still recognized Him. He walked, talked, and ate with them several times before returning to heaven. More than once, He appeared when they were in locked rooms, which suggests that He materialized before their eyes. When a doubting disciple questioned Him, Jesus said, "Touch me and see; a ghost does not have flesh and bones, as you see I have" (Luke 24:39, NIV). If your heavenly body will be like His, then you will still be flesh and bone, and you will walk, talk, and eat, plus have miraculous powers.

God created the earth and everything in it, including the angels. Everything has a purpose. The angels are ministering spirits. God never said that when you die you would turn into an angel. This is a false assumption, perhaps arising from the idea that a spirit without a body would float. But Jesus disproved that existence when He said He was not a ghost.

"He will change our weak mortal bodies and make them like his own glorious body" (Philippians 3:21, GNT). Although no one knows exactly what the heavenly body will be like, the Bible does give you some thoughts about it. The promise that God gives, and the one you can count on, is that you will be like Jesus.

worth thinking about

▶ **God's followers** will possess two types of bodies: a weak, earthly one that will die and decay, and a heavenly one, which will never die.

▶ **In eternity**, you will have a heavenly and spiritual body like Jesus'.

▶ **The Book of Revelation** says that heaven is filled with beautiful sights and sounds. There is constant activity, and you're invited to a wedding supper. Surely your heavenly body will be enriched with even keener senses than your earthly body.

> *We will put on heavenly bodies; we will not be spirits without bodies. . . . We want to put on our new bodies so that these dying bodies will be swallowed up by life.*
> 2 Corinthians 5:3–4, NLT

question

Does God promise heaven to everyone?

God is the Creator of the world and everything in it. God's goodness has always been a given for you. You have personally experienced His goodness on more than one occasion. But the other day, you were at a loss for words when a friend asked why a good God does not send everyone to heaven. You know God has His reasons, and you know He is good, but you weren't prepared to explain it. Are there specific scriptures you could have used?

answer

God's goodness is evidenced by His continual care toward His creation (Psalm 104). Everything He does is for the sake of His created. You, along with the rest of creation, are very important to God.

Even God's laws came into being because of His goodness. His love for mankind is immeasurable. He desires that you live a peaceful life free from the pain of wrong choices. God realizes that obedience cannot be forced, for then it is not the result of love or respect. Again, He acts in goodness by giving you the freedom of choice.

God is good, but also holy—perfect and honorable in every way. Heaven is the place of perfection where He lives. When Adam and Eve broke God's laws, death and decay entered the world. The punishment for sin, breaking God's law, is separation from God. The Bible says everyone has broken His laws at some point.

God in His goodness offers a new covenant promise, one that can keep you from being eternally separated from Him. He sent His Son to pay for your wrongdoing by dying in your place. This gift of grace, which you do not deserve, is God's goodness at its best!

The goodness of free will is offered to all. Those who say yes to God's gift have all their wrongs wiped away. They can come into God's presence. Those who turn down the free gift and say no are also saying no to heaven.

worth thinking about

▶ **The choice of** where a person spends eternity is an individual one. God won't decide it for you. "If we refuse this great way of being saved, how can we hope to escape?" (Hebrews 2:3, CEV).

▶ **God in His** goodness instructs everyone in His ways (Psalm 25:8).

▶ **God's goodness** is fair and patient. He waits and waits, giving you time to choose life. Psalm 145 says He is good to all and has compassion on all His creation.

> As surely as I live, says the Sovereign LORD,
> I take no pleasure in the death of wicked people.
> I only want them to turn from their
> wicked ways so they can live.
>
> Ezekiel 33:11, NLT

Readers who enjoyed this book will also enjoy

100 Answers to 100 Questions About God

100 Answers to 100 Questions About Loving Your Husband

100 Answers to 100 Questions About Loving Your Wife

100 Answers to 100 Questions About Prayer

100 Answers to 100 Questions to Ask Before You Say "I Do"